TRUE O

· The husband smilingly assures his worried wife that he would never fool around with another woman. The wife is relieved. Her man will never stray.
True or False?

· You've got your quarry in a corner. She's so confused, she answers your payoff question with both a spoken "yes" and a negative shake of her head. The woman is obviously lying.
True or False?

· He's the very model of passionate conviction. His promises are laced with prefaces like "Let God strike me dead if I'm lying. . . ." He's got to be telling the truth.
True or False?

· A man unconsciously calls his companion by another woman's name. It's a deadly slip—a sure clue that he's never been able to get the other woman out of his mind for a moment.
True or False?

The answers are inside this book. Many of them will surprise you. And that's no lie!

THE LIE DETECTION BOOK

William J. Majeski
with Ralph Butler

BALLANTINE BOOKS · NEW YORK

Library of Congress Catalog Card Number: 88-92151

ISBN 0-345-35565-2

Manufactured in the United States of America

First Edition: January 1989

To Evelyn, my wife, for her patience and wisdom.
To Nicole and Julie, my daughters, for their views
on life and their imagination.

CONTENTS

THE
LIE
DETECTION
BOOK

CHAPTER

1

A RIGHT TO KNOW

ONE NIGHT MY WIFE AND I WENT TO A PARTY WHERE the only person we knew was the host, a fellow named Hank. As he introduced us around, he mentioned my profession, warning everyone not to waste time lying to me. "He'll catch you," Hank said cheerfully.

Nobody paid much attention, except for a serious young actress who thought this was a great challenge. She came over, her blue eyes wide, and asked me exactly how I did what I did. My wife smiled.

"Oh, that's a trade secret," I replied, trying to discourage shoptalk. But the actress was into her own professional skills, and after some more banter she got to the point.

"I don't think anyone has ever caught me in a lie," she said.

By then, several people were listening, so I decided to perform a little magic. Hank's eyes gleamed. My wife drifted into another room.

I asked the actress to sit in a chair. "Think of a number from one through ten," I said. I handed her my business card. "Now write down the number and hide it in your hand."

Then I told her that each time I mentioned a number— any number—she should look at me and answer, "No."

She agreed. I stood facing her, a few feet away, and slowly proceeded from one through ten. Something told me it wouldn't be easy this time. She had an audience, and she was an actress.

At two, she looked at me, nodded her head, and said "No." Tough! At three, she folded her arms, closed her eyes, and squeezed herself before replying. At five, her eyes opened wide, and she blurted out her no. At six, she shifted in her seat, feigning nervousness. "N-n-no," she stuttered. At seven, she bit her lips before murmuring. At ten, she crossed her legs, then recrossed them, nearly purring the last no. She was very good.

Then I said, "The number you wrote down is five." And I immediately regretted it.

Her triumphant look vanished abruptly. I thought she might burst into tears. But, thank heaven, she regained her composure before turning up her number.

It was five.

The onlookers made some noise then. Hank chuckled.

"How did you know?" the actress asked me, half pouting, half demanding.

"Because when you said no to number five," I told her, "you lied."

"But how could you tell?" she insisted.

I promised her it would all be in my book—as soon as I wrote it. She wasn't at all mollified. But she was smart. It wouldn't surprise me if she has most of it figured out by now.

How can you tell when someone is lying? I can't count how many times I've heard that question—from clients, young cops, amateur sleuths—in my twenty-one years as a security expert.

But the answers are not simple. In my world detecting a lie is an art form.

In your world, too.

Our moral horizon has lowered. Few will argue that point, although the change could be more a matter of scope than substance. I doubt human nature has changed.

Chances are that a lie rose from the heart to the mind to the lips just as easily fifty years ago. But there are a lot more lips now. In 1940 the population of the United States was 131 million. Today it is 250 million. And with the advances in our communication technology, including the flood of talk on TV, there are many more words gushing.

More truth, inevitably. More lies, undeniably.

Regardless of what you do in life—at home, in school, at a party, in a relationship, in politics—you're aware that lies are flying high and low. Competition for space, power, and wealth is fierce on this crowded planet. If a lie means an edge, many people will lie.

When you're conscious of it, a lie's impact usually depends on how much it affects you. It may not matter one iota. And when you're oblivious, the same weight applies. The damage depends on what's at stake.

But when you're unsure, the cost can be heavy indeed. Suspicion, unresolved, becomes a corrosive force. Doubt destroys trust.

Some philosophers will always preach that truth is relative. We are even told that a judicious lie can be a good thing.

Fine. But to those who believe it is acceptable or even advantageous to lie, you have the prerogative to say:

- I want to know when people are lying to me.
- I want the option to accept or reject those lies.
- If I can avoid being vulnerable to a lie, I want a way to avoid it.

This book, then, offers you a method for detecting lies.

CHAPTER 2

THE FIVE CLUES TO LIE DETECTION

I JOINED THE N.Y.P.D. IN 1967. MY FIRST TWO YEARS were spent in uniform walking a beat and driving patrol cars at the West 126th Street station in Harlem. Those were my only two years in uniform.

Then came a six-year assignment to the district attorney's squad in Brooklyn as an investigator of white-collar crime and organized crime—my first daily experience in one-on-one lie detection. In 1971 I was promoted to detective.

In 1974 I was sent to the National Polygraph Training Center for a course in polygraph science. I did testing for the D.A.'s office, refining such basic skills as question formulation and what to watch and listen for in an interrogation or interview.

I was transferred to the narcotics division of the Organized Crime Control Bureau in 1975 and was involved in long-term drug investigations in Manhattan for most of the next seven years. I also caught my share of homicide investigations. The most notorious case involved tracking down Jack Henry Abbott, the convict-turned-author now serving a life term in state prison.

My polygraph work in those years incorporated both law enforcement testing and a good deal of work in the private sector. I conducted seminars for the 125-member New York State Polygraphists Association, serving as president from 1978 to 1980. The next year I became the chief instructor at the New York Institute of Security and Polygraph Science.

In 1982 I was reassigned to the Brooklyn D.A.'s detective squad, investigating organized crime, white-collar crime, and political corruption. I remained there until my retirement from the N.Y.P.D. in January 1988, after twenty-one years on the force.

Today I own an investigation agency, Majeski-Klein Associates Inc., specializing in corporate intelligence. As you may have guessed, one of my specialties is lie detection.

When I was asked to put some conclusions from my years of frontline experience into a book, I thought it would be a good opportunity to help solve what many people regard as a mystery—and to do it in plain English. Lie detection is a maze, but it's no mystery.

So, without further ado, let's take it from the top.

There are five major areas in learning how to detect lies. Classification can be endless, but these are the basics. I call them The Five Clues.

CLUE #1—*The Zoom Focus*. How to watch closely for the ingredients of a lie. A simple way to recognize facial expressions, body language, gestures: the Silent Signals.

CLUE #2—*The Funnel Effect*. How to listen effectively to what often goes unheard. A system for picking up Sound Signals: vocal tones, sudden changes, unconscious sounds, word choices—and silence.

CLUE #3—*Matchups: Signals and Words*. How to compare Silent Signals and Sound Signals to the words spoken. Are they consistent or is there some conflict?

CLUE #4—*Spare Thinking Time*. How to evaluate the progress of a dialogue while you're listening—or while you're talking. A strategy for staying one step ahead.

CLUE #5—*Searching Questions*. How to proceed when someone is evading an issue. A subtle method for excavating that elusive answer.

In the chapters that follow I will explain in detail how these clues work—and how you can use them to detect lies in everyday life.

CHAPTER 3

HOW THE FIVE CLUES WORK

TALK IS SUCH A BASIC FORM OF HUMAN CONTACT THAT we wonder why it sometimes seems so difficult. But if you look and listen closely, you can see why. And hear why.

For me the best opportunity for that kind of study comes when I'm out of town on business. That's when I spend the most time alone in a crowd.

Not long ago I sat by myself in a fine restaurant, idly snooping as the other patrons ate, drank, and made conversation. From a distance it looked as if all the talk came easily and smoothly, just as it does in the movies. But I learned long ago how deceptive that can be.

I began tuning in to a middle-aged couple at the next table. The husband didn't have much to say, verbally. At intervals the wife would make a comment, so low I couldn't quite hear. He would grunt. When she asked a question, he responded with a shrug or a wave of the hand.

Then her voice rose slightly. "I did," she said, shaking her head. And that triggered what for her husband was a torrent of words. "No, you did not," he said. "You never told me."

I tuned out then. I didn't want to hear any more. One gesture had signaled where the truth lay. Do you know what that Silent Signal was? Well, you will know soon.

Conversation is a far more intricate puzzle than most people perceive. Let me briefly outline all of its components.

Words would seem to carry the most weight, but not for me. Spoken words are mixed with a complex array of Silent Signals that can be much more powerful.

These signals have their own variables. They can be blatant or subtle. They are isolated or in combination form—simultaneous or consecutive.

A smile and a nod with the word *yes*—that's a simple amalgam. Or there can be a blizzard of gestures, facial expressions, body language, and stray sounds—all combining into what is technically known as nonverbal communication.

That's a term that you will come across fairly often. I call these aspects of communication Silent Signals because *nonverbal* can be a confusingly negative mouthful. But it's accurate enough because all the components—limbs, body, head, eyes, face—have different functions. The nonverbal aspect is unifying, all-encompassing.

Amid the mixture of words and signals, there is also a nearly constant conversational switching between the roles of talker (or sender) and listener (or receiver). When you are trying to get information or detect a lie, you need to play both roles.

Complex, indeed. But it's a familiar puzzle, one you confront each day, and I assure you there is no trick to its solution. Most of the answers you seek—when you suspect someone is lying—are there to observe, right out in the open.

Detection comes with accurate interpretation of what you observe. Since accuracy rests on knowledge repeatedly applied, I have devised a simple process for spotting almost any lie that comes your way.

Here are my Five Clues to Lie Detection. Seek them, and you should find the truth.

THE ZOOM FOCUS *(Clue #1)* teaches you to look for specific visible signals. I will tell you just what to look for, the full catalog of signals—far beyond the mere smile or frown. If he can't sit still, if she wrings her hands, if his Adam's apple bobs—that kind of Silent Signal will leap out at you. Once you're zeroed in, the signal becomes magnified. And if it's significant in context, you will know it.

THE FUNNEL EFFECT *(Clue #2)* sharpens your hearing so that your ears become highly sensitive antennae when a potential lie is in the air. I know of no better system for gathering evidence of falsehood without regard to the words being spoken. If the tone rises or lowers, if there's a Freudian slip or a sudden silence, you'll pick it up.

MATCHUPS: SIGNALS & WORDS *(Clue #3)* will train you to assess what you have seen and heard. Matching a Silent Signal with a spoken word is the logic of lie detection. If the two components don't match, you look for some degree of deception. Finding inconsistency is the challenge.

I am going to raise your consciousness notch by notch. In only a few days you will realize that no matter what form a nonverbal signal takes, it is rarely incidental or accidental. While words can be controlled, few facial expressions are contrived. Gestures and tone are usually spontaneous. Most body language, as you will see, is utterly unconscious. Psychiatrists read it every hour. So can you.

SPARE THINKING TIME *(Clue #4)* is the essential element in all forms of productive communication between people. It is fundamental to most of our favorite competitive pursuits, from poker to baseball to chess, because it helps you to think ahead. And yet, despite the obvious value of Spare Thinking Time, it is usually wasted.

While some succeed in evaluating what they hear, few are aware of the spare time they have to plan ahead while talking. If you know how to read your audience, you can produce information from even a trivial dialogue. A negative can turn into a positive. You learn to react with more certainty, to control situations—and perhaps events. You can save your business, your marriage, your life.

SEARCHING QUESTIONS *(Clue #5)* provide an organized method of digging for answers that seem stubbornly elusive, possibly because they're deliberately hidden. My follow-up quiz—a package of specific probes in a given order at stipulated intervals—has turned up the truth for me in many security cases, extracting answers from unresponsive people. If you ask the right question at the right intervals, that stony façade can crumble. It works—whether you're trying to detect a fact, an idea, an illusion, character, passion . . . what is true and what is not.

CHAPTER

■■■ 4 ■■■

CLUE #1—THE ZOOM FOCUS

THE WORD *OBSERVE* HAS AN ELASTIC QUALITY TO IT. You can be an active or passive observer. You can glance at people's faces, or you can study them. You can see their gestures and body language clearly or be dimly aware of some fleeting movement.

Our range of observation is wide, but it almost always depends on our need to know. Normally we see only what we want to see.

In viewing Silent Signals, that range is more than adequate. Be willing to look. That is your only responsibility. I promise you that you will be looking for something very specific. And don't worry about being a neophyte. You have more experience than you realize. A magnifying glass or telescope brings a specific object closer when you want to see it more clearly. The zoom shot in photography achieves the same goal.

But now you are going to use your eyes alone, with

a sharper focus than you ever imagined. You can train yourself to see something specific every day—often in a situation where someone might want to tell a lie, and you want to detect it.

Zoom Focus will become as instinctive as looking for oncoming cars, examining a peach for bruises, watching an umpire call balls and strikes, or checking a lover's face to see what kind of mood he or she is in.

When you suspect that you are listening to a lie, you will begin to see a pattern emerging. And then you will discern a change in the pattern. It could be the first real clue.

Not always, of course. You must take circumstances into account. Physiological factors, for instance, can play a role in any communication. If someone has just been punched in the face, his rubbing the spot would be natural. It loses any other meaning as a gesture.

But when a lie is possible, zero in. Look for Silent Signals. Matching them with the words spoken will usually tell you just how much those words are worth.

Just as you enhance your physical health with exercise, you can sharpen your powers of observation.

For starters, watch people while they're talking.

Practice studying the faces of people in conversation everywhere—at a party, in your office, in a restaurant or bar, on a bus or train.

If you're at an airport ticket counter when a flight is delayed and an airline spokesman explains why, study the expression on his face for signs of distress. You're not likely to find one; airline spokesmen are adept at masking distress. But if he does show any such signal, the crowd will ask plenty of questions. Signals act as triggers.

In a retail store watch a salesman make his pitch. The good ones will look saintly but otherwise expressionless. They are determined not to convey doubts about their merchandise with the wrong signals.

When you watch people talking, whatever the setting, try to assess the situation—friendly, angry, neither, or both. If you can hear their actual words, fine, but just observing their mannerisms is enough for a start. If words are the bricks of communication, nonverbal signals are the mortar.

What sort of signals do you seek? Ah, here is the beginning of the maze. Let's walk through it.

For your first step, watch for the most familiar facial expression: a smile. You will now start collecting smiles—carefully, as if you were collecting butterflies.

You are not looking for lies, not yet. Look for variety. You will find an amazing spectrum of smiles. Broad smiles, thin smiles, nice or nasty smiles, pained or ecstatic, fleeting or semipermanent, nervous or practiced, diabolic, sarcastic, toothy, automatic, inappropriate . . . . People show many, many kinds of smiles.

Collect them, wherever you go.

TV is the most fertile field I've discovered for collecting smiles. For watching all kinds of signals, to be sure, but particularly smiles. There's an almost Pavlovian reaction, I think, for people who know they are on camera. Unless their front teeth are rotted, they smile.

Watch TV talk shows and interviews, from Johnny Carson's or Barbara Walters's to *60 Minutes* or your local talk-talent from Boston to Miami to Seattle. It's an endless garden.

A helpful note: In the early stages, it is wise to turn off the sound on TV. You're trying to concentrate on smiles, and the spoken word is a distraction. So, for now, just watch.

The Zoom Focus is an exercise in concentration, and studying can be a problem in a variety of circumstances. My solution is to focus your attention in somewhat the same way you do while cooking a meal or driving a car. It's just a matter of getting the job done.

Some tasks are more difficult and require more concentration. Performing brain surgery. Teaching in an unruly classroom. Flying a plane. Hitting a golf ball straight. Hitting a baseball *at all*—how do they do it?

The Zoom Focus can seem impossible until you have practiced it diligently—and have trained yourself to concentrate. That's what doctors and teachers and pilots and athletes do. They are looking for results.

Now it's your turn.

Zoom in.

Make notes of your butterfly collection of smiles— mental notes when you're in public, and written notes as soon as you have the opportunity. When you're by yourself on Sunday morning, tune in to the TV talk shows. Watch all the smiles. Practice with the sound down for a while; then turn it up.

When you see a really striking smile, record the circumstances in writing—primarily the type of smile, but also a brief notation of who smiled and why, along with any pertinent dialogue if you heard it. (Sample record: Toothy, man of fifty, politician, mild joke.) Situations are really secondary, though. What you want to isolate here, chiefly, is the type of smile.

Remember, the goal of Clue #1 is to learn to observe visually and retain what you see. You will retain more than you think because the Zoom Focus provides a photograph in the mind. In time your collection of mental images will help you to identify each of the Silent Signals listed on pages 19–22 in separate catalogs of facial expressions, gestures, and body language.

When you have practiced gathering smiles for a few days, start collecting at least three examples of each of the other Silent Signals . . . from frowning to toe tapping.

That's the complete drill for mastering Clue #1. If you want to stretch yourself and jump ahead of the class, just be alert for inconsistencies—any signal that does not match the situation or the words spoken. Some expressions or movements will be clearly inappropriate, maybe due to obvious emotional stimuli. But in my catalog of Silent Signals you will find the seeds of effective lie detection.

Gradually, watching people will pay large and steady dividends. After a week you will be considerably more observant than you were yesterday. After two weeks you will be alert to nuances that may seem elusive now.

In a month, with very little effort, you will pick up each of the Silent Signals sent almost constantly, not only by strangers but by people you know well.

EXERCISES

1. See how many variations you can observe of each of the signals listed below.

2. Make your own estimate of whether the signal was normal or unusual at the time you observed it.

3. Was it generally *consistent* with the circumstances as far as you could determine—or did it seem *inconsistent*?

Go ahead. Evaluate these Silent Signals one by one.

FACIAL EXPRESSIONS

smile
frown
smirk
laugh
sneer
breaking of eye contact
squint

FACIAL EXPRESSIONS

stare
raised eyebrows
dilating of pupils
closing of eyes
rapid blinking
startled look
worried look
face losing color
open mouth
tight lips
sticking lips
biting of lips
biting of cheek

GESTURES

nod
headshake
touch
hand wave
wringing of hands
hand stop sign
covering eyes
covering mouth
showing palms
making fist

GESTURES

pointing finger
scratching head
rubbing face
cracking knuckles
picking lint
swatting fly
steeple gesture
tapping fingers
playing with fingers

BODY LANGUAGE

head bowing down
head turning away
heavy gulp
rapid breathing
dry cough
nervous tic
shoulder shrugging
arms folding
arms stretching
wrists crossing
hands opening and closing
body slumping
restless body (anthill sitter)
body shrinking away

BODY LANGUAGE

leaning back
leaning forward
legs crossing and recrossing
feet pointing away
toes tapping floor

There you have not all, but certainly the most common signals. There's nothing inviolate about my list. If you observe a stray signal that interests you, just add it to the list.

Situations where Silent Signals seem inconsistent with the circumstances are legendary in public life—and no less memorable in private.

There is a classic photograph of John V. Lindsay, former mayor of New York City. He had just been asked a tough question at a City Hall press conference. Like most politicians, Lindsay normally wore a poker face. But now, thinking hard, he instinctively put a hand over his mouth and squeezed—with so much force that his handsome face was contorted.

"I'm glad you asked me that question," Lindsay finally said.

The place broke up.

Covering the mouth is a gesture you will observe often when someone wishes to bottle up the truth.

* * *

Let's say you're a single woman at a party, standing alone. A man approaches, making conversation. Sooner or later, if you're interested in him, you're likely to ask: "Are you married?"

If he says no, he might be single. But just in case he's lying, there will be subtle clues to the lie.

Watch for a nearly imperceptible half nod of the head before he says no. The combination of a *no* and a half nod translates into a probable *yes*.

Why? Because the half nod was obviously unconscious—and that tends to be more truthful than the conscious.

If he is looking directly at you when he says no, watch to see if his eyes close or if he looks at the floor. Either movement can represent a denial of the word *no*. Keep watching.

Does he raise a drink to his lips or otherwise cover his mouth while saying no? The gesture requires exploration. If he shifts his feet or plays with his tie before answering no, he may just be excessively nervous—or he may be very married.

If he makes a joke ("No, do I look married?"), you could consider the response witty. But it's a diversion at best, and at worst it's an evasion.

If your new acquaintance professes his bachelorhood with three or more such contradictory signals, and you doubt his veracity, you're on solid ground.

A real no requires only the word *no*—nothing else.

How many times have you watched this one in your office?

"Do you mind taking care of this report?" the boss asks his partner's secretary. "My girl is out sick."

"No, I don't mind. No problem," the secretary says, smiling and nodding. (She really doesn't mind.)

"No, I don't mind. No problem," the secretary says, unsmiling, arms folded, looking at the wall. (She minds.)

This scenario fits a variety of situations.

It's rumored that a co-worker named George is passing company secrets to a rival firm—a possible case of industrial espionage. You ask him about it.

"Don't give it another thought," George says while picking lint from his lapel.

"Cut it out, George. We've been friends—"

George raises a hand as if to stop you. "If we're friends, don't ask me a question like that," he says.

"Don't worry," you say, "I'm not going to tell anybody about this."

George begins to crack his knuckles, then seems to come to a decision. "What do you want to know?" he asks, rubbing his chin.

Is George about to speak the truth? Not from the evidence. There have been too many defensive tactics on his part.

Hand movements, in particular, can contradict what is being said. While someone is telling a lie, he may use a hand to cover either his eyes or his mouth— sometimes his whole face. It's usually an involuntary sign that he's denying his words.

* * *

A husband smilingly assures his worried wife that he would never consider fooling around with another woman. His words are welcome enough, but why the smile? Since this is a threatening situation for the wife, his smile seems inappropriate. It's a signal to her to accept his words with no further questions. Even if it's unconscious, the smile is probably motivated by guilt and a desire to cover it up. What's significant here is his timing. The smile shouldn't come until after she accepts his words of assurance—not before.

A boss is quizzing a salesman about the status of several pending orders, most of them routine. It's purely an update session, and both men maintain natural eye contact. Suddenly the boss asks about a really important order: "Did you get it?"

The salesman, who knows he's not going to get the order, glances down briefly, then looks up. "I think so," he says. "I talked with the guy. He's considering it."

An alert boss will dig deeper. Let me explain why.

It is not always important for someone to look you straight in the eye. Born liars can gaze at you unblinking for hours. Honest people may need a moment to compose what they want to say.

But it becomes important when someone looks you in the eye until you ask a direct question and then glances away.

A tip-off is a glancer's deadpan stare, his looking straight at you immediately after he has glanced away for a split second under pressure. That sequence of signals is persuasive evidence of a lie.

* * *

"Don't give it another thought," George says while picking lint from his lapel. That's an excerpt from the industrial-espionage anecdote cited earlier.

Why is it a signal of deception when someone picks lint? Well, it isn't—not in itself. People may remove lint from their own or others' clothing for no other reason than tidiness. But anyone should be studied closely if he begins lint picking at the same moment he answers a direct question.

This particular activity becomes significant when it's a form of avoidance, a reflection of being uncomfortable. The person involved seems to be saying: "I'd like to answer your question but I'm so busy picking this lint off me that I can't answer you right now." It really means that he can't answer the question honestly—and that he needs a moment to think of a believable response.

What makes the lint-picking gesture revealing is that more often than not it's imaginary lint. It just doesn't exist. I've seen people under stress pull off tufts of material when there was no lint.

Tapping fingers are a sign of nervous tension. A lot of people drum their fingers or crack their knuckles as a lifelong habit. Some play with their fingers.

There's nothing inherently suspicious about any of these traits—unless they are inconsistent with the normal pattern. Ask anyone, for instance, how much money he makes. Here's what might happen:

1. He has not drummed his fingers until then, but suddenly starts.

2. He has been unconsciously drumming his fingers until then, but suddenly stops—or starts to drum faster.
3. With no known history of knuckle cracking, he abruptly cracks his knuckles.
4. He grabs one of his middle fingers and starts rubbing it. (If it's a woman, she slowly twists her ring.)

It's all unconscious and, in truth, quite innocent. But you will have to take their responses with a grain of salt.

Why? Because each of them changed his pattern before (or while) answering a direct question. And the inconsistencies cropped up under pressure, at a moment when an exaggeration was possible.

Income is a measure of status in our culture, so many people will lie their way up the ladder. But some will dilute their real worth, just in case you're asking for a loan.

So, watch those fingers.

Touch can be more powerful than words—for positive or negative effect. There's a whole science developing now on the general subject of touching and the role it plays in human relations. In terms of lie detection, we can reduce it to this:

A boss who pats a worker on the shoulder occasionally will encounter less resistance when a question of truth arises. A parent will experience the same phenomenon with a child—any genuine show of affection increases the honesty quotient, sometimes dramatically.

· For the purpose of detecting truth, the negative side

of touching emerges when the show of affection is disputable—as often happens with an idle pat on the head or backside, or when a person touches just for the sake of touching.

There are some who have a particular reason to lie— who think they can profit by it. They might save their lies for special occasions. Then there are those who lie just for the hell of it. They practice the art all their lives, so they're better at it than ordinary people. Some liars are born into it, with a mastery of what is regarded as charm, or seductivity.

It's really no more of a skill than picking pockets, but we've all known people like that who fool us . . . for a while.

Police informants are known for being psychopathic liars, often unreliable in sensitive investigations. You can't trust them, but their tips often have such deep implications that you have to follow them up. I've found many informants useful. All you have to do is watch them.

One was called Johnny Boy.

I first met him in late 1983 when a Brooklyn retailer told us that some fast-talking rip-off artist was trying to buy $4000 worth of electronic equipment with a credit card. There had been a flood of phony credit cards that winter, and stores were getting hit hard.

Johnny Boy was hitting stores. He was twenty-two, married, with two children and no job, but he liked high living—and he had access to a few stolen credit cards. I offered him the opportunity to cooperate.

He was a little excited about it. He thrived on different kinds of excitement. What I wanted were his sources, and he eventually led us to eight thousand fraudulent cards. We made eight arrests, including two soldiers in the Gambino crime family.

For more than two years Johnny Boy lied all the time, about everything. He would talk in half truths. The more he lied, the faster he wagged his tongue and the faster he moved his hands and body. A lot of people slow everything down when they're lying, but Johnny Boy got excited.

I learned to read him quickly because of this acceleration of movement when he lied. If he spun his hand twenty revolutions per minute in normal conversation, he spun it about forty rpm during a lie.

Yes, it's that simple. It's fairly easy even for an amateur to detect someone's normal pattern. What's significant is inconsistency—any changes from the norm. Any of the Silent Signals below can be normal or abnormal, depending on the context.

Changes are more muted in most liars—glancing away from you, covering the eyes or mouth, for example—and Johnny Boy was inclined to do that, too. But most of his changes were exaggerated, like the hand spinning.

I just looked at him. After a while he used to put his hands in his pockets when he talked to me, but it didn't do any good. His shoulders and elbows were still moving unconsciously during a lie.

When trapped Johnny Boy turned on the hyperbole, but not too convincingly. He was notorious for that hackneyed oath: "I swear on my mother's eyes." His blind mother.

But if it wasn't going to cost him too much, Johnny Boy got a kick out of being caught in a lie. He would glance down at the sidewalk very sheepishly. Then he'd look up and grin.

Informants are not ordinary people. Most of them are street-urchin types who survive by their wits. They are excellent readers of body language, so they can figure out what people want to hear, and say it. They have a keen unconscious sense of when an intended mark is agreeing with them. The mark might smile, or nod, even move the lips slightly—as you do when you start to say *uh-huh* but don't vocalize it.

Sometimes listeners will relax their bodies slightly, perhaps a signal that they accept what you're saying. Street people like Johnny Boy will pick up on that.

Why do ordinary people miss these signals? They're not paying attention. Maybe they're administrators bogged down in work or housewives distracted by their kids. No matter who you are, it's easy to become oblivious.

It takes some effort to notice Silent Signals.

CHAPTER

⬛⬛⬛ 5 ⬛⬛⬛

CLUE #2—THE FUNNEL EFFECT

MOST PEOPLE LISTEN TOO CASUALLY. I WOULD SAY carelessly, except that in some cases the laxity is deliberate. Often we don't want to hear all the words that bombard our ears, so we tune out.

There's nothing inherently wrong with preferring oblivion, but I question whether that's what the casual listener really wants. The reality is that tuning out requires a fine touch. Without the touch you miss too much.

Casual listeners don't know how to concentrate when they need to concentrate. They miss information, true or false, and they can't easily tell the difference. They have difficulty remembering exactly what was said.

How much do you miss?

The true barometer is: How much do you retain of a conversation or discussion you had yesterday—or even an hour ago? How much of it do you remember? More than a few words? Think about it.

To listen effectively requires awareness.

"Pay attention now. What I'm going to say is going to be very important to you," I warn my lecture audiences.

That command heightens their awareness.

But it's not necessary to wait for a command. You can give yourself the same awareness.

Are you ready?

The Funnel Effect is my most important lesson in teaching students how to listen more consciously.

Picture an ordinary funnel (like the one in your kitchen). At one end it's wide, at the other narrow.

Normally we listen through the wide end.

But to listen intently, you must listen through the narrow end.

Here is an illustration of how to use Clue #2.

Turn on the radio news and make a conscious effort to concentrate on what you're hearing.

Absorb one sentence, of about a dozen words, accurately.

Do it again, and then again. Extend yourself to hearing two sentences accurately. Then four.

You can almost visualize the funnel narrowing.

At a party, eavesdrop on some of the animated conversation you hear. Usually when you eavesdrop, you're listening just enough to decide whether it's a dialogue you want to join.

This time, remember the Funnel Effect.

Listen to each sentence carefully, absorbing each

word. But in this exercise you have an added purpose: to absorb the content.

Is it light conversation about upcoming vacations or children's activities, about baseball, about the weather?

Is it more serious and structured? A discussion of the presidential election, the better home computers, the drug menace, AIDS, the federal budget deficit?

If it is a dialogue with substance, listen to hear if people are responding to what's being said or are introducing their own messages.

If one person seems to be neither listening nor responding appropriately, ask yourself whether he doesn't comprehend what's being said or if he's changing the direction of the conversation.

If he is introducing something new, is it a useful diversion? Is it forceful, or weak, or unintentional?

And so on.

Your goal is not only to absorb what you hear, but also to comprehend it more fully. And regardless of the content of the conversation you tune in to, I guarantee this: You will be amazed at how much of the dialogue you will be able to recall tomorrow—with utter clarity.

Now, let's carry the Funnel Effect one step farther.

At a business meeting a decision is to be made on the future course of the company, on a new product, or on a change in the focus of a sales campaign.

Even if you're an experienced hand at group meetings, the thread of several crisscross arguments can still get lost. Worse, you can get bored. And once boredom hits, listening stops.

Instead of sitting idly, however, try this: Pipe into the narrow end of the funnel. Purely as a honing exercise, listen with extreme concentration. Don't waste your time. Put Clue #2 to use.

Evaluate the force of each argument—and of your colleagues—in terms of the words and approaches used. Who gets the upper hand? Why? What seems to work? What doesn't?

See if you can predict which argument will be accepted by the man or woman at the head of the table.

Tomorrow you will be impressed by how much of the meeting's substance you are able to retain. Yes, whether you want to or not.

Since words are usually chosen for their effect, they are the conscious part of the speaker's message. Words are relatively easy to control. But there are innumerable unconscious Sound Signals that are an integral part of nonverbal communication.

And just as you learn to absorb words using the Funnel Effect, you train yourself to absorb signals the same way.

The history of experience with lost senses shows what you can do.

How do blind people function? Many claim development of a sixth sense, basically an intuitive antenna, especially for danger. Of necessity they become acutely sensitive to movement and language, much more sensitive than people with eyesight.

The blind will hear inconsistencies in vocal tones or sounds that the rest of us rarely hear, unless we are properly using the narrow end of the funnel.

This is important. You learned the concept of inconsistency in Chapter 4 and will encounter it often in subsequent chapters. But nowhere does the idea carry more weight than in hearing vocal tones and sounds.

It is not the tone or sound itself that matters. It becomes important only when it is inconsistent—discordant, jarring to the ear, a wrong note.

An automobile engine suddenly misses before regaining power. A baby cries for a brief moment in the night. A stairway squeaks in a horror movie. A doctor with a stethoscope hears an irregularity in a heartbeat. These sounds are inconsistent. And it usually matters enough to listen more closely.

When someone is talking, if you hear an inconsistent sound, listen more closely.

Vocal tones vary from person to person, but each individual usually speaks in a steady tone. What becomes significant is the moment when that steadiness varies, creating a tonal distortion, if only for a split second.

There are cases where a change in tone is pronounced and prolonged—as when someone becomes angry or hysterical. The change is distinct then, and the reason for it is probably obvious.

Momentary changes (the meanings of which will be explored in Chapter 6) are what you should concentrate on here—the brief distortion that serves as a signal.

Here is what to listen for:

1. *A rise or fall in pitch (or register)*, especially if it is quickly corrected. When a voice switches from low to high and then back to low, something is probably wrong with what's being said.

2. *Changing rate or rhythm of speaking*, as when someone interjects a brief staccato burst of words into an otherwise steady monologue, or changes his usual conversational rhythm and sustains the change. It's the sort of change that occurs when one is humoring someone, or avoiding an issue, or practicing deceit. If a normally gruff person suddenly becomes more open, or a gushing type abruptly withdraws, it's almost certainly a signal that anyone would try to decipher. But any change in rate or rhythm is worth pondering.

3. *Force*, the strength applied to a single word or phrase. Force can convey more meaning than a speaker intends, because emphasis is usually unconscious. It doesn't count for much when a politician emphasizes a word like *unity* in his oration while briefly mumbling the word *taxes*. But in normal conversation, knowing what provokes a more (or less) forceful tone could be important.

4. *Cracking voice*. When there is no physiological reason for it, people's voices tend to crack because they are afraid or excited—aroused in some manner, either pleasurably or unpleasurably. Telling a lie can be one cause, but not the only one. Think about all possible causes.

Sounds are at least as important as words—often more so—because sounds are nearly always unconscious and therefore uncontrolled. An instinctive, unrehearsed sound is likely to convey more truth than the prepared, well-formulated phrase.

A cessation of sound might also tell you something, often something false. For example, when your direct question is met by hesitation or a slight pause or even a hum, brace yourself.

"So, how long have you been divorced?"

"Six, years. How about you?"

"I just broke up with someone."

"Ready to try again?"

"I'm in no rush. I'm afraid of getting hurt again."

"No pain, no gain."

"Oh, yeah? So how come you haven't remarried?"

"Uhmmmmm . . ."

That's what I call a hum. Any sustained tone like that, in lieu of an answer, figures to be a stall. What is the hummer hiding?

Silence is deafening, as the saying goes. Tell an arson suspect during an interrogation that you are going to ask him a hard question. Tell him you want either a truthful answer or none at all.

Then say: "You set that fire, didn't you?"

If he set it, chances are he will sit there in absolute silence.

Always hear what a person does not say, especially when it matters.

MOM: What time will you be home from the dance?
TEENAGE DAUGHTER: Around midnight.
MOM: Good. Will Douglas be driving you home?
DAUGHTER: (with a groan): I'm not sure yet.

That groan, purely instinctive, certainly matters. It signals deep resistance to the question and loads the daughter's unresponsive words with unconscious meaning. Could it be that the truth would require a change of her plans?

I would say that if your daughter's safety is at stake, Mom, ask more questions.

A real estate broker, Joe, has a loud arguement with the bookkeeper over his expense account. The boss summons Joe and asks, "What's going on?"

Joe gulps, then tells his side of the story. It is a detailed response, but the boss should not discount Joe's preliminary signal.

The gulp says the question was hard to swallow. Could it be that Joe was padding his expense account?

If you hear a slight stammer or slurring and if it's uncharacteristic, pay attention.

WIFE: Why aren't you coming to the party?
HUSBAND: Cause I-I-I've gotta lot of work to do. . . . I, uh, it's important . . . the, uh, boss, um, wants it tomorrow morning.

That kind of answer just raises additional questions. Why isn't he more coherent? What is he hiding?

Ordinary words and phrases might take on different meanings each time they are used, even by the same person. The differences can be heard in the tone, inflection, and emphasis.

"You look wonderful," someone says. A nice compliment, perhaps. In fact, it can be sincere or sarcastic—depending on how it is delivered.

While the effectiveness of words might depend on the cleverness of the speaker, their impact also can come from the sensibility of the listener.

Everyone is vulnerable to the impact of certain words. I call them Helium Words.

Helium Words have a particular effect. Words like *sex* or *money* or *death* create universal impact. In our time the words *AIDS* and *nuclear* seem to have taken on similar weight. In a less heavy vein are nouns like *love* or *depression* or *dinner*.

A Helium Word causes your concentration to float away.

College professors don't use the word *sex* in the classroom on a spring day. Too distracting.

Money is a topic that can make people's eyes glaze, whether the focus is on spending it, earning it, losing it, or marrying it.

The reaction triggered by many racial or ethnic slurs makes them Helium Words. So are derogatory nicknames based on physical traits.

Helium Words are not limited to a single word. They encompass a single thought but are often expressed in a phrase or clause.

Thank God it's Friday is one example. *My mother-in-law is coming over.* . . . Essentially, that's just another Helium Word.

The largest category of Helium Words is personal. They distract different people at different times for intensely personal reasons. Your Helium Words depend on what's important to you. The association can be positive or negative. In either case it's almost always unique.

I know a man who used to work nights. He's been on the day shift for ten years. But still, the phone can ring at 7:30 P.M. and a friend will ask: "Asleep?" It drives the guy up the wall. Helium Words can have that effect.

In childhood, Helium Words that bring us pleasure are used by our parents to delight us. In later years, words that disconcert us are used by family and friends to delight themselves. Just a fact of life.

Choice of words and word sequence are rarely accidental. They're employed to deliver specific messages, sometimes without regard to the truth.

Deception, in the telling of lies, is so blatant that phrases jump out at you: "I swear on my father's grave. . . ." "Let God strike me dead if I'm lying. . . ." When someone is making that much of an effort to convince you, it's a cover about ninety-nine percent of the time.

Wrong use of words should set you thinking. How often have you heard a Freudian slip laughed off by everyone in the group? It can be funny, of course, and often it's innocent. It can also reveal something important: an unconscious blurting of one's true feelings.

I have seen instances of a man and a woman in conversation, where the man unconsciously calls his companion by another woman's name. Does that mean he still feels strongly about the other woman? Probably.

But it doesn't necessarily mean that he feels that way all the time. Should the feeling have been suppressed? Yes, but he slipped.

That's why Hollywood types and other prudent people address each other as *dear* or *honey*—like Zsa Zsa Gabor, who simply calls everyone *darling*.

How do you become aware of what's important in a person's voice—not to mention the cascade of sounds we hear every day?

Start your research on the telephone. It's the easiest place to limit outside distractions. If necessary, place a hand over one ear so you can hear better.

Tune out all interference to intensify your concentration. Closing your eyes can work wonders.

Absorb each word. Mentally record a sentence with total accuracy. Then two sentences, then three. Listen for inconsistencies, as you do unconsciously when a conversation is of special importance to you. For practice, start doing it all the time. You'll be surprised how quickly you will start picking up signals you never heard before.

People think of a telephone as a shielding device. They are more inclined to lie over the phone, where they think facial expressions are not a factor.

But if you are listening for it, you can learn to *hear* a smile or a frown. It's easier to hear a smile, as you're aware when salespeople make a phone pitch. They're trained to send you an unseen smile; they've tested the power of it many times. A smile translates into a much more profitable sales curve.

With practice on the phone you will pick up any

human emotion that transmits visually. If you have an answering machine, replay conversations. You may hear more than the caller intended.

And watch TV talk shows—as prescribed in Chapter 4, but this time with the sound up. Listening closely will let you analyze both cause and effect in the interplay of words and Sound Signals.

Concentrate on the choice of words and word sequences employed by both the host and the guests.

When you hear something that jars you even slightly—an inappropriate response or the wrong use of a word or a Freudian slip or any inconsistency—make an estimate of what it means. You don't have to be right, not at this stage, although usually it's a simple give-and-take on TV, with nothing of significance hidden. And whether or not your estimate is on the mark, the exercise will bring you fuller comprehension of more complex dialogue.

> Here is a memory bank of Sound Signals for ready reference: word choice, word sequence, change in rate (speed), change in tone, change in pitch, cracking voice, Freudian slips, overpersuasion, sudden stammer or stutter, slurring, grunting, groaning, moaning, gulping, snorting, sniffing, humming, whistling, teeth grinding, hesitating, pausing, silence.

Collect examples of each of these Sound Signals by using Clue #2, just as you collected Silent Signals by using Clue #1. Make a written or mental note, depending on the circumstances, when you hear anything uncharacteristic: a random stutter, an odd choice of words, a sharp change in tone or pitch, and so on.

Because nonverbal signals tend to be fleeting, after the first week you should chart what you hear. Start a file of three- by five-inch index cards and record each Sound Signal you collect. Include a brief note of the context whenever possible: who delivered the signal—and why.

Paying close attention to vocal inconsistencies helped me solve a retail theft case in Pittsburgh about a year ago. Here's what happened:

The store's cash registers were being steadily ripped off. Small amounts of cash were missing, but many falsified credit slips were being written for phantom goods which supposedly had been returned to the store. The total discrepancy came to about $3,000.

The entire staff consisted of ten salespeople, including the manager and an assistant manager. The boss was mystified, without any idea who the culprit was. The assistant manager suspected one salesman who seemed to be "throwing around money"—spending much more than he earned. Other employees had noticed that, too.

Suspicion is a funny thing. It must be carefully assessed. Six witnesses will suspect someone who turns out to be completely innocent. Usually it's either the result of a personality conflict, or else the real crook is sowing mass suspicion to deflect attention from himself.

One woman expressed suspicion of another salesgirl

who she said had acted "nervous" after being questioned by the manager.

"What do you mean, nervous?" I asked.

"I don't know," the woman replied vaguely. "Cindy just acted strange." Like most people, she could only sense that something felt wrong. She couldn't pinpoint it.

I decided to interview Cindy first. We sat alone in the manager's office and had a lengthy talk. I kept it low-key because Cindy was reluctant to talk. She was indeed excessively nervous, so jumpy that she qualified as what I call an anthill sitter.

A twenty-one-year-old college junior working part-time, she fidgeted while I filled out her background form. I talked slowly, stretching out the conversation until she calmed down a little.

"Now, let's talk about the problems the store's been having," I said, deliberately offhand. I wanted Cindy to set the tone. And she did, immediately.

A small guttural sound came from deep in her throat. She was choking down her words before they came out.

"I'm not . . . sure . . . of . . . what problems?" she said haltingly. And that first signal immediately got my attention. The fact that Cindy was avoiding the issue at that early stage was significant.

"You're kidding," I said with a smile. While I had to let her know I had picked up the signal, I didn't want to alienate her.

"Oh, you mean the money that's missing," she said.

"Well, that's good for starters." I kept smiling.

Cindy said, "I was told some money was missing, but I don't know anything about it."

Her right arm twitched a little. The elbow jutted out, warding off attack. Her body language was subtle at this point, nothing dramatic—but easy to interpret.

I asked what she had heard.

She looked at me and started to open her mouth, but she had difficulty parting her lips. They made a popping sound. She croaked: "I don't know."

I backed off even further, asking some idle questions about her job responsibilities.

The white-hat approach? To some degree, yes. But let me tell you, the white hat stays on virtually all the time with most detectives. Your position must remain: I want to help you.

This time it paid almost instant dividends.

Cindy slowly explained her store duties: helping customers, ringing up sales, cataloging layaways, straightening garment racks, keeping track of inventories—all routine duties.

The part she omitted was my first major signal.

She never mentioned writing a credit slip for a customer—a common activity, and perfectly legitimate. Cindy was too intent on avoiding that subject.

Theoretically, nobody except the two bosses was authorized to write credit slips. But when the bosses weren't there, the salesperson had to do it. So I asked Cindy directly if she ever made out credit slips.

She hesitated, looked away, gulped, wet her lips—there was a tremendous amount of hesitation.

"Well, uh, I'm not allowed to make out, um, credit slips," she finally stammered.

It was almost over. I asked who okayed a credit slip when both bosses were out to lunch. Her legs crossed, then re-crossed. She said, "Whoever's there."

Had she personally ever written a credit slip? "Well, er . . . I guess I did." She tugged her skirt down.

Cindy was a hem puller. The closer we got to the truth, the closer her skirt got to her knees. It wasn't a prepared act. It was involuntary, like a snail going into its shell.

"Did you at any time fill out one of those credit slips and keep the money for yourself?"

She blushed. "No, I wouldn't do something like that." Her voice was cracking.

"Why not?" I asked.

Totally confused now, she was unable to think of an answer. She shook her head, and then whispered, "Because."

All right, it's a cat-and-mouse game. It's not always nice, but it doesn't have to be nasty. And when you need to know the truth, you have to play the game expertly. I then asked a two-part question: "How many slips have you filled out"—I paused, so she could think—"and then kept the money for yourself?"

Cindy was silent after the first part, thinking. And after the second part, she kept on thinking! Her silence spoke volumes, though, and finally she felt the trap.

She didn't get angry. Just flustered. She looked at me wide-eyed, then looked away. "I don't understand what you mean," she said.

"Look at me," I said, "and I'll ask you again."

This time I asked the question with no pause. Cindy bent her head and studied the floor.

"None," she said. Still no anger.

Her voice belied her words. There was a lack of forcefulness in her denials, an inability to maintain tonal consistency in explaining her activities, and her evasive response to questions.

"I don't believe you," I said. No response at all. She was mute.

My ears were picking up more than enough signals now—all inconsistent with Cindy's story. Since there was no longer any question about the truth, I wanted to get to the meat of it. I told her: "Think about what you're going to say. It's just a matter of us getting together and agreeing on what happened."

Cindy said: "I don't know what coulda happened." She seemed to have revived a little.

I offered her my hand, figuratively. I explained why it would be better for her to admit the truth. "I'm here to help you. So let me help you," I said.

She sighed heavily. "Well, I want you to help me."

It still took another twenty minutes. We talked about her strong religious beliefs, her education, her major, her professors, and the fact that I teach courses, too—drawing the only common bond we had.

Intermittently I would touch again on the issue of the missing money. I asked Cindy how much her tuition was, and how she had been paying it.

"I earn some of it at the store, and my parents help me," she said. So we talked about her parents, who were separated. She looked unhappy discussing her father. I switched to her aspirations for the future. Cindy said she she wanted to go into business.

"It's going to be tough with something like this hanging over your head. Do you want that?"

"No."

"Let's talk about it."

"Okay."

For a while she would admit only to falsifying credit slips "two or three times" for a total of $150. It was far short of the missing $3000. When her full confession emerged, piecemeal but accounting for all the missing money, she wept with remorse—and relief. A nice girl. When she left she said, "Thank you very much."

Cindy signed a statement promising full restitution. The store chose not to prosecute her. She was dismissed for "not adhering to company rules."

If you know what you're doing, a polygraph test usually won't be necessary. I try to determine that right away in an interview—to find out if the subject is going to be cooperative or not. Sometimes that can be tricky. You can ask accusatory questions, but once you make a direct accusation, you're into what is called a *power interview*. I try to avoid the power interview because it can arouse emotions. That creates physiological stimulation too excessive to allow a fair polygraph if testing then turns out to be needed.

No test was necessary when I heard one of the classic Sound Signals in my experience. It was emitted by a thirty-two-year-old bartender named Harry, who sniffed and snorted like a horse.

Harry had spent ten years learning his trade before he landed in a lower-Manhattan bar near the financial district, where business was usually brisk.

After six weeks of Harry's bartending, the owner realized his profits were being diluted. But when he spot-checked the alcohol content of his open stock, there was no sign of dilution. I was summoned privately just before Christmas to solve the mystery.

"What's going on?" I asked Harry in my usual friendly way.

"I don't know," Harry sniffed. "The owner's complaining business is down. I don't know what his problem is. Maybe it's the holidays, people saving their money for [snort] Christmas presents."

To accompany the snort, Harry raised the right corner of his upper lip just as a horse would do. It facilitates the snort. I wondered what it signified.

We talked about customer flow, what kinds of regulars came in, how the tips were—innocuous subjects. I was looking for inconsistencies, but Harry was straightforward and cooperative.

I tried silence for fifteen seconds. Harry sniffed. "Listen," he said, "this is bullshit [snort]. Every time business goes down, they have to blame someone."

"Are you stealing from the register?" I suddenly asked.

"No," Harry said. There was no sniff.

"Maybe watering the stock?"

"No."

"Any other way you've figured out to steal the man's profits?"

This time I heard Harry grind his teeth slightly during the question. His *no* was as decisive as usual, but sure enough, he lifted his right lip slightly and snorted.

It was uncanny. A clue? Well, I decided that with two inconsistent signals (grinding and snorting) in response to one question, the response probably was a lie.

I bounced back to noncontroversial subjects: Harry's previous jobs, his opinion of the owner, the fastest-moving brands. . . .

"Hypothetically," I said, "if you were going to steal from this bar, how would you do it?"

Harry grunted. "I've been bartending for ten years," he said. "I've never stolen anything." (But he hadn't grunted before, either.)

"Are you kidding?" I grinned. "Don't all bartenders steal?" (Between the two questions, Harry gritted his teeth.)

"That's a lot of bull [snort]," he said.

The signals were thicker now, so I zeroed in.

"Did you ever bring your own bottle here, Harry?" I asked softly.

His only response was a snort, with the lip curled.

The way it worked, as Harry eventually confided to me, was that he would bring in his own twelve-dollar quart of a popular brand of vodka.

Every other drink he sold came out of his bottle, which contained thirty-two ounces of real booze. Each shot weighed an ounce and a half, so he sold twenty-four drinks as sort of a private entrepreneur—and never rang up the sale on the register.

At $3 per shot, Harry pocketed $72 for a $12 bottle of vodka. No wonder the owner's profits were down.

Why did Harry confide the truth to me? Because when he snorted at my question about the bring-your-own-bottle trick, I changed the subject.

"Do you have any mannerisms," I asked, "like twisting your neck, or cocking your head, or snorting?"

"No," Harry said honestly enough.

"Are you playing the bring-your-own-bottle trick?"

"No [snort]."

"You just snorted," I said quietly.

"No, I didn't."

"You did. Every time you lie, you snort. Watch. Did you bring your own bottle?"

Harry had to restrain himself physically from snorting.

That posed a dilemma for him—dealing with the twin realization that he had an unconscious habit and that he had been caught lying. He remained silent, but he was upset. You could see him going through the mental process of denying it and grabbing his face to see if he was snorting.

It was truly a radical experience for Harry—confronting something of which he had been unaware.

I promised him that if he told me the truth, I'd tell him how he could eliminate the habit of snorting.

He told me the truth.

I explained to Harry that he was already halfway to

the solution of his problem—awareness. All he needed now was the conscious effort to control it.

He asked: "How?"

I told him to keep an eye out for this book.

■■■ 6 ■■■

Clue #3— Matchups: Signals & Words

You are awake, out in the world somewhere, mixing with people. With nearly every tick of the clock, you can pick up a nonverbal signal. You recognize it now. You have seen it or heard it before, several times. You have collected it.

What now?

The next step is to determine whether the signal was consistent with what's being said—the spoken words. Did they match or were they inconsistent in some way?

Was the inconsistency revealing? What did it tell you? The answer will be Clue #3.

Now that you know how a Silent Signal is transmitted, you learn how to interpret it.

This is not an exact science, not any more than medicine is. Lie detection isn't always $1+1=2$. But when it comes to interpreting a message, I'd rather study a few unguarded signals than any number of words, every time.

Words, obviously, can be controlled. So can a few superficial looks, like the practiced smiles of movie starlets and sports heroes that seem to flash on and off so casually.

But facial expressions are not generally easy to contrive. Most gestures and sounds are spontaneous. They ring with truth. And for perhaps ninety-five percent of the human race, body language is utterly unconscious.

You can depend on Silent Signals with confidence, as long as you remember that nothing is automatic. Avoid making rote judgments. Some signals will carry less or more weight, depending on the circumstances. The importance of your own mental and emotional perspective will be discussed in Chapters 7 and 8. And physiological factors play a role in anyone's responses. If someone has a chest cold, for example, it reduces the significance of a cough. If you know someone is on drugs, their effect should be considered. Don't ignore any qualifying conditions. Evaluate them.

While steady concentration is required at times, it will be worth it.

If you recall my "magic" experiment from Chapter 1, your concentration level is high. Try the experiment yourself, preferably in a well-lit area so you can see into the other person's eyes.

Here's how you arrange the experiment.

1. Ask the subject to think of a number between one and ten. He is merely to concentrate on this number, not divulge it to anyone. (Let's say, for example, that he thinks of five.)

2. Tell the subject to say "No" each time you say a number aloud. Make sure he is concentrating.

3. Slowly proceed from one through ten, speaking each number aloud. Watch the person's eyes carefully as he responds, "No."

4. If the *pupils dilate* in response to a direct question, it's a reliable sign of lying. (In our sample case, then, the subjects pupils should dilate when you reach five.)

Eye movement is central to interpreting what someone is saying. The mouth area is almost as revealing, but the eyes really have it. If the eyes close as the mouth answers, you'd better rephrase the question and try again. If they close again, it means the person is hiding something.

It pays to give attention to such seemingly mundane factors—and not only in party games. Silent Signals often reveal facts of serious consequence.

A mother reads a newspaper story about a drug problem at her son's junior high. Four students were arrested on charges of selling marijuana inside the school. None of the juveniles are named.

Her son Tommy is fourteen. The mother has mixed emotions. She doesn't want to know if any evil has touched her son, but she needs to be certain.

She decides to mention the subject during dinner

that evening. After some small talk, she comes to the point matter-of-factly, hiding her deep anxiety.

"Tommy," she says, "there was an article in the paper about a problem at your school—about pot being sold."

The boy keeps eating. "Yeah," he grunts, offering no clue—or at least no helpful response.

The mother glances sharply at him and demands, "Do you know anything about this?"

Looking down at his plate—still eating, a little faster now—Tommy reluctantly concedes the obvious: "I heard somethin'."

The mother blurts out, "What did you hear? Do you know any of the kids involved? You're not smoking pot!"

Now the boy looks at her. He stops eating, slumps slightly in his chair, and seems to shrink away. "Everyone in school is talking about it," Tommy mumbles. But with his mother staring hard at him, he decides to talk.

He sits up and starts talking faster. "There's just a few kids involved. I don't know any of them personally, but I used to see them hanging around. Three or four kids. I'm not friends with any of them. They're not my friends."

Many parents would gratefully drop the subject at this point. They would be effectively reassured for the moment and unwilling to dig for more facts. When the truth could be painful, they settle for evasions.

That's exactly what happens to Tommy's mother. His flood of denials ends the conversation—but should it?

Were there enough Silent Signals from Tommy, despite his denials, to justify further questions?

Absolutely yes.

By giving curt answers and shrinking away from her questions, Tommy was clearly trying to avoid them.

The accelerated rate of his denials meant that he was anxious to bury the whole topic of pot.

And most important, of course, was the fact that Tommy never answered his mother's most important question—probably because it wasn't put in question form.

She should have asked him: "Are you smoking pot? Have you ever smoked pot?"

His reply to such direct questions would have told the mother what she needed to know—or possibly what she dreaded hearing. In any event, she would have done her teenage son a favor.

As things stand now, she still doesn't know the answer.

His silence was deafening. Her silence spoke volumes. Mere clichés? Of course not. The Fifth Amendment has demonstrated the validity of such metaphors.

When you hear nothing in response to your direct question, even if it's merely a hesitation or slight pause, brace yourself for anything from an evasion to a whopper.

And if it's dead silence, no more words are needed.

Try telling a steady boyfriend (but be sure he's sober) that you are going to ask him a question—that you want him to think about it seriously—and that you want either a truthful answer or no answer at all.

Then say: "We're not ever getting married, are we?"

If there's a long silence, that's your answer.

When you're applying for a job, the personnel manager will ask why you left your last job. If you were fired but don't want to admit it, try to avoid uncrossing and recrossing your legs before answering. If he knows his business, he'll know you were fired.

If she's anxious to leave, she will sit with her feet pointed toward the nearest exit. When she says, "I haven't decided how long I'm staying," just check out the direction of her toes.

You and your husband, Harry, are scanning the menu at a new restaurant. Harry can't decide, so he asks the waiter, "What do you recommend, the meat loaf or the pork chops?"

Harry is still peering at the menu. You watch the waiter's face. He glances upward and frowns with distaste, then responds: "Well, sir, the meat loaf is very popular tonight."

The waiter's signals tell you that there's still plenty of meat loaf left in the kitchen. You advise Harry to try the pork chops.

It's sound advice. The percentages are that you're right.

Some good-looking women will try to vamp you. They've seen flirting work in the movies, and they have tried it with some success. But it rarely works when they're trying to hide something wrong.

I remember a vamp we'll call Debbie. She was twenty-seven, a very attractive little blonde out of Kentucky, with Dolly Parton measurements but no voice. In warm weather she hung out near a big hospital on Manhattan's East Side wearing short shorts and a halter. She did a little hooking and was into drugs, but nothing major.

One night a police drug-buy went haywire because the dealer swiped the cash from an undercover cop and ran. We pulled in everyone in the area for questioning. That's how I first met Debbie.

I wanted to know if she knew the pusher, a guy named Sammy, but my questions were routine. You can't give everyone the third degree—at least not right away.

Debbie said she had come from a girlfriend's apartment. She had stopped to buy cigarettes at a candy store and was just leaving when all hell broke loose.

"I saw a lot of men running and some of them had guns," she said. "I got confused and ran back into the store."

She seemed truthful and looked very comfortable sitting in a chair in my office with her legs crossed. I asked how much she knew about what had happened. She leaned toward me and smiled radiantly.

"I'd just left the store," Debbie said.

Alarm bells clanged. Not only was she denying personal knowledge, she was claiming a noninvolved position—and selling her claim with body language.

Debbie's positive radiance was Clue #3—inappropriate to her negative message.

"You were there for a while," I said. The undercovers had told me that much.

"What do you mean?" Her voice rose a notch.

"You were standing there in the doorway."

"Yeah," Debbie said, watching me.

"What were you doing?"

"I was just watching some people arguing. I couldn't figure out what was happening." She looked at the wall.

I decided to break the pleasant routine. I told her she was full of it; she knew exactly what had happened outside the store.

The legs uncrossed and recrossed nervously. The bare shoulders drew back, not so friendly now. She just folded her arms, forgetting about using her body and personality to act as Miss Innocent.

We fenced for forty-five minutes. She denied knowing Sammy. She insisted she wouldn't lie about such a thing. On and on.

"Look me in the eye and say that," I challenged her.

Debbie tried. She leaned toward me again, took a long breath—and smiled. It was no use. Her vamp act was over. "Yeah, I know Sammy," she said.

It turned out she knew almost everything that had gone down—a superb witness. And it didn't end with that drug case. She became a valued informant.

Why?

Well, she loved excitement, and there was a certain thrill in it. Also, Debbie didn't have much in life, and

I became a person she could talk to. She gravitated to that, and she couldn't pay me in drugs, she couldn't pay me in sex.

So she repaid the obligation she felt to me in information.

Women are usually more animated and emotional than men, so that can make men easier to read. Women will mix up the signals a lot when they become flirtatious—which some even will try when they're being truthful. Usually I make a pronouncement early about my wife and kids, and that stops that with the honest ones. Usually.

It's not a simple equation, but most of the time a flirtatious woman (or man) is just trying to attract attention—nothing more.

I once gave a polygraph test to a young shoe salesman named Frankie. At twenty he was assistant manager of a store where the stockroom was set afire. The marshals called it arson. The store manager wanted lie tests for all the employees who were present.

In his pretest interview Frankie crossed his legs and thrust out his chest. He spoke in a high register. I noted that and discounted it, because he was answering most of my questions quickly and unwaveringly.

But he couldn't sit still—a typical anthill sitter. And sometimes, when it mattered, he answered too methodically. When I asked if he had gone into the stockroom before the fire, Frankie closed his eyes briefly before answering no. Then he gave me his deadpan stare.

Does that seem familiar? You're right. It's a prime example of the essence of Clue #3.

I was at least alerted that Frankie might flunk the polygraph test. When he did, and I gave him the bad news, he shifted in his seat again, gulped a few times, and looked out the window. When he spoke, he almost whispered.

He said: "I don't know why the machine said what it did. I honestly had nothing to do with the fire."

I felt strongly that Frankie wanted to admit he had struck the match. I tried several different tacks to open him up. But I couldn't find the right formula, so finally I told him I had other work to do. I said, "I don't want to waste any more time with you, so I'm going to ask you to leave."

Then I saw panic in his eyes. He slumped backward, gripping the armrests of the chair. I knew he wanted to confess.

I opened the door. "I'd like to have helped you," I said, "but you're not letting me, so please go." Frankie cowered in the chair, without a sound.

I grabbed him by an arm, but he wouldn't go. "I've got more important things to do," I said. I took both his arms, lifting him out of the chair. With effort I ushered him out the door. I closed it.

I didn't hear Frankie walk away. When I opened the door, he was standing there crying.

"Do you want me to help you?" I asked.

I offered my hand. He took it gratefully. I led him back inside.

After some more tears, we talked. He said he had started the fire because he was angry at the shoe company. They had brought in the new manager from another store instead of promoting Frankie.

He wanted to express his anger—but nobody else knew what he had done except him. Confessing was his announcement to the world.

This can get overanalytical, but Frankie's confession might have been a form of bragging. And bragging is an effort to relieve the anxious tension of knowing something nobody else knows. The bigger the secret, the greater the tension.

Do you know something not known by anybody else in the world? Most people can't keep a secret to themselves. They have to share it with someone.

And while it's relatively easy to keep a secret as long as no one's inquiring about it, it's not so easy when you're asked a direct question. It introduces a new stimulus: the opportunity to tell what you know.

It's a circle. All communication is a circle.

CHAPTER

■■■ **7** ■■■

CLUE #4—SPARE THINKING TIME

ONE METHOD FOR READING PEOPLE AND STUDYING situations is to slow down.

S-l-o-w d-o-w-n.

When your thought processes are in control, your thinking is orderly.

You consider the consequences of your words and actions.

You evaluate the other person's posture and make adjustments if necessary.

Successful communicators do this every day.

John F. Kennedy had a ploy to give himself time to think about a tough question.

"Let me say this about that," President Kennedy would say, stalling for time.

The ploy eventually brought laughs at JFK's press conferences. And that gave him even more time to think out his response.

* * *

I call it Spare Thinking Time, my fourth clue to controlled observation, and there is no more valuable commodity in the field. It has little to do with the ticking of a clock. It gives you a strategy for exerting control—and in lie detection, for creating an opportunity to find the truth.

It draws on power you may not even know you had. Even if you are someone who normally becomes very thoughtful before speaking, there are times when anyone will talk without thinking. You can control that impulse, since you have the power to think much faster than you talk.

You have the capacity to think faster than a speeding bullet if it's coming straight at you—as many survivors of close combat will attest.

And you can certainly think faster than the flow of words coming at you.

Our brains, which operate with the speed of an electrical impulse, give us generous stretches of Spare Thinking Time. Most people do not use it. Some exploit Clue #4 unconsciously, but not to its full potential. They tend to use it only when something is important to them—for a job, for love, for life itself.

The trick is to use Spare Thinking Time at will.

You train yourself to use it—to think before talking, while talking, and while listening. It can help you to control a conversation, perhaps to control events. And to the degree that it helps you find the truth, it allows you to *win*.

That's why Spare Thinking Time is a staple of any game, skillfully played. At the poker table, for example, being able to read people makes a difference.

You associate actions and reactions; you keep track of how someone plays a good or bad hand. Observing how a card player reacts to a series of bad hands, noting any change in the player's physical activity, will tip you off if the hand becomes good. Normal reactions to cards fit into a pattern.

Creatures of habit find it hard to cover their tracks.

Once I got involved in a poker game at a picnic to help a friend recoup a $400 loss. I don't play that much poker, but after watching the five other players at his table for a while, I thought I'd see if the cards were running my way.

Two of the five players were pretty sharp, and winning big. A third was about average, breaking even. The other two were weak, unwittingly tipping off the value of each hand they were dealt.

But all five showed me several quirks.

Player Number One had a clear voiceprint. When his cards were bad, he drew replacements quietly and bet in a soft tone if at all. With stronger cards his voice was noticeably more forceful, and his calls were accompanied by a tiny nasal hum: "Mm." You wouldn't hear it unless you were listening.

Number Two was a squinter. His eyelids would close tighter, like Clint Eastwood's, when his cards were good. And he would snap a card with unconscious gusto if he liked it. If not, you wouldn't hear any snap.

Number Three held valuable cards with all ten fingers tucked underneath so he wouldn't drop anything precious, like a full house. He held valueless cards with one hand underneath; the other skimmed along the top, fishing for a hidden ace. He would ante up with an overhand motion when he had something—but just pitch in his money when he had nothing.

Number Four was a squeezer at draw poker or stud. He would carefully separate his cards, whether five or two, by squeezing them apart. If they were any good, his eyes would widen and he would bring his prize closer to his chest. If he held a high pair in draw, he carefully isolated them. If he held three cards and drew two, you only had to watch his face on the draw to know the result. He either flashed a faint smile or a look of disgust. No control at all.

Number Five wasn't much better. If he drew the right card, he immediately put his hand on his money, ready to bet. If not, his hand never went near his money. If he tried to bluff me then, I felt confident because his initial reaction had been negative.

With the help of some decent cards, I recouped my friend's losses in a few hours. The cards have to be there, but the difference between winning a little or a lot at poker consists of reading the other players.

You look for patterns and then watch for inconsistencies. If there is no clear pattern for any one player, it must be deliberate, so beware of him. Some poker players are so well versed in negotiations that they can create an illusion of loss of control and use that against their opponents.

But keep looking for a chink in a player's armor. Everyone has some unconscious patterns, because we are all creatures of habit.

* * *

I once dueled for hours with a chemical engineer. (Let's call him Archibald Harrison III.) It was my all-time favorite game of wits, even though my opponent thought he won it.

I didn't agree.

Archibald Harrison III was an academic high-achiever type in his middle thirties. Poised, smiling, and articulate, he was well regarded and handsomely paid by the huge firm that employed him. Not your typical crook.

Someone in the firm and a cohort outside created a fictitious company of their own, a wholesale chemical outlet. The inside man shipped merchandise—fifty-gallon drums of a chemical product—to an address in a deserted warehouse area. But it was just a transfer point—with the outside man quickly moving the merchandise elsewhere. At first Mr. Outside promptly paid the supplier's bills—about $10,000 per shipment. Then he ordered a $50,000 shipment.

This time there was no payment. Mr. Inside merely fed false information into the supplier's computer. He specified that the $50,000 shipment had been returned as the wrong substance. That established credit for a second shipment. So now the plotters had $100,000 worth of chemicals, costing them nothing. A few weeks later they ran their $50,000 game again. Finally they hustled a $75,000 shipment. Then they quit.

Computers, more and more, are silent accomplices to larceny. There is limited accountability, with no signed paperwork—so it can take months for a supplier to spot discrepancies. By the time the supplier hired me as a private security consultant, the loss totaled $350,000.

The supplier identified five highly placed employees who had had the authority to pull off this scam. Each readily consented to a polygraph test.

Archibald Harrison III was among them.

He was a familiar type to me in a pretest interview. Assured, self-contained, undemonstrative. Very subtle gestures, often covered with a smile or a laugh.

"Look," I said, "we've got $350,000 credited to a fictitious company listed at an empty storefront. Can you shed any light on this?"

Archibald put his hand over his mouth and said, "I really don't know." Then he smiled—and my antenna went up. The hand gesture, after my first specific question, was something to ponder. But the smile was definitely inappropriate. It wasn't consistent with what was being said.

Harrison smiled a lot. He used his smile as a mask when he thought his face might be revealing something. He was extremely cautious, a person who was well drilled in the duel.

At my prompting he outlined his responsibilities in the firm.

I asked: "That would give you ample opportunity to do something like this, wouldn't it?"

Harrison crossed his legs. "No, not really," he said. Then he uncrossed his legs, putting both feet flat on the floor again. A little nervous? Naturally. But ill at ease? I wondered why.

I gave him the polygraph test. Harrison failed it.

His physiological responses were markedly incon-

THE LIE DETECTION BOOK

sistent. He was smart enough to know that, too, but he made no physical attempt to distort his responses. He didn't tighten his stomach muscles or flex his arm. He didn't move any part of his body. He knew that would be recognized as deliberate distortion, tantamount to deception.

Harrison later admitted that he had done a lot of reading on the subject of polygraphy. He understood that a confession was my goal. And he had no intention of confessing.

To open his post-test questioning, I told him bluntly that he was the guilty one—that he was the one who profited from the whole scheme. While I talked, he started to nod his head involuntarily. But he caught himself—and smiled.

Then I said: "I've got bad news for you. They've found your partner, and from what I understand, he's talking."

Suddenly there was panic in his eyes. The pupils were dilating and the eyes grew larger. Not for long. For two seconds. "Not a chance—" he started to blurt out. But he recovered his poise in time, and said, "You're crazy. I don't know what you're talking about."

He had just stopped himself from challenging the truth of my claim that his partner had turned. He hadn't admitted he had a partner.

Archibald was smart. I complimented him on his brightness. He praised my technique. And we dueled for three hours. He stuck around all that time for the challenge of it. And he won—because I didn't get a confession.

But I did get confirmation. At the end, when I told

him he had won, he got up and left, slowly closing the door behind him. Eight seconds passed. Archibald opened the door a crack and poked his smiling face through it.

"You almost won," he said.

No tracer was put on the lost money. It wasn't a police investigation, so the case never was officially solved. As far as I know, Archie and his pal just walked away with $350,000.

That they embezzled it, I have no doubt.

I've administered thousands of polygraph tests. I've never made a mistake that I know of.

The moment of truth is not always predictable. When it comes, do you challenge or conciliate? Ask or demand? Apologize or deny?

By being able to use your Spare Thinking Time, you are prepared for any eventuality. Let me illustrate:

You walk into your boss's office and say, "Boss, I've got to have a raise!"

He responds in one of three ways:

1. "What makes you think you deserve a raise?"
2. "I really can't give you a raise right now."
3. "I doubt that's going to be possible. Let me think about it."

Your task is to observe his response and evaluate it, so you can decide whether to pursue the matter, or bide your time pending developments, or drop the subject.

Some of the variables are institutional: the company's size and financial health, the boss's autonomy, his job security. Others are subjective: your determination, the force of your argument, your importance to the boss—and your ability to adjust to his response.

There was a lot of hedging in the boss's language. Was there an apologetic gesture—did he turn his palms to you? Did he lean forward and smile sympathetically? Did any combination of Silent Signals indicate that a raise was worth pursuing? All these considerations deserve pondering.

Nobody knows better than you why you merit a raise. It's possible the boss doesn't actually know. Tell him what your value is. If you can't identify it, how can you expect it of him?

If he can't give you a raise right now, when can he? Try to get a future commitment from him. At least it will give you an inkling to his sincerity.

The boss's third response was the trickiest—both negative and positive. But since he proposes to think about it, give him something substantive to consider. Your reaction itself, if calm and reasonable, could be the best way to persuade him of your worth.

After all, the boss never did say no. The door has been left open. Don't let frustration overwhelm you. There are many times when a decision appears to be going against you but then the situation changes.

Skill at using Spare Thinking Time pays financial dividends, large or small. You notice the payoff when you go to market—especially for big-ticket items.

I needed another car recently and went out to see what was available. There was a station wagon I liked in the front row at the local used-car lot. The discounted price on the windshield was $13,500.

"How much is it really worth?" I kiddingly asked the salesman who appeared at my side as if by magic. He didn't answer my question directly for quite a while.

"Hey, this baby is only a year old, only twelve thousand miles, and it's always been garaged," he said, watching me to see how I'd respond. I shrugged and looked skeptical. It behooves you not to smile too agreeably.

"A one-owner car, a little old lady who really pampered it. Look at that interior. It's in mint condition," he raved in the usual enthusiastic tone. "And everything under the hood . . ."

I gazed into the distance, as if looking for another used-car dealer. The guy was almost physically leaning on me now, encroaching on my space, exerting pressure. That's a tried-and-true sales technique—to move toward you. It's a distraction, and it could distort your judgment.

"I see some dents," I said, pointing at a few of them. "What about the accident this little old lady had?" It was a clean car, but to make sure, I wanted to see his reaction. Someone denying a valid accusation will move away from you, putting distance between himself and guilt.

"No, absolutely not," the salesman said, not moving. I took that as a positive sign, and decided to negotiate.

I said, "Tell me the truth. I want your rock-bottom price."

Very few people use the word *truth* with high-pressure salesmen, so they're not accustomed to hearing it. Some can be knocked off balance by the inference that they have not given you a final price.

"I can let you have it for, oh, twelve-five," he said.

"Well, I'm interested, but I want to hear your lowest price," I said—knowing I hadn't heard it yet.

All I had heard were two signals.

First was his choice of words. He used a positive construction ("I can let you have it for . . ."), which left room for further negotiation.

A negative construction ("I can't let you have it for less than . . .") would have been stronger, more definitive—and closed the door to further negotiation.

Second—just as important—the words *twelve-five* were spoken in a distinctly lower tone than the start of his sentence. It was the change in tone that interested me. The *twelve-five* wasn't forceful. That meant he was hopeful but not certain.

Now, when I insisted on hearing the bottom line, he shuffled some papers in his hands. "All right, but I can't go any lower than $12,000, and that's my final price," the salesman said quickly and smoothly. His hand sliced the air with finality.

I smiled and nodded. His words and his tone and gestures were consistent now. That balance made me comfortable. I bought the wagon.

When does final mean final?

Let's put it this way. Final means final when you feel comfortable with what is being said. The reality is that you might have felt comfortable when he was saying $13,500, but I contend there has to be more communication than that.

Unless there's a dialogue, you're depriving yourself of finding out whether a salesman is telling the truth or not—and possibly of a chance to save money.

In this case it was $1,500.

EXERCISES

To sum up, here are six methods by which to put your Spare Thinking Time to work.

1. Catalog people's traits.
2. Analyze the content of what is said (by them and by you).
3. Recognize inconsistencies.
4. Calculate your possible response in any given situation.
5. Send your own nonverbal signals, with a specific message.
6. Master tact!

Let me elucidate:

1. Cataloging traits is a simple exercise in observing, identifying, and retaining some of a person's mannerisms. Not all. Some. The process becomes worthwhile when one characteristic constitutes a

signal, as you learned in the previous chapters.

At the poker table, I needed to identify the traits of each player—how he normally reacted to good or bad hands. In order to keep track of which player displayed which traits, I made mental notes. Number One was a hummer, Number Two a squinter, Number Four a squeezer, and so on. That's what I mean by cataloging.

Follow the same course when you're dealing with anyone, especially when sizing up strangers whose traits aren't familiar to you.

2. To analyze the content of what's being said, you don't have to be a psychologist. Just listen to the words and sentences through the narrow end of the Funnel—remember? Absorb the literal meaning, with the help of any signals you pick up. Here's where your new antenna become priceless, because human dialogue is not always crystal clear by any means. You need to analyze it with some accuracy.

   Then you can prepare your response with some care. If it's clear that someone is trying to manipulate you, resistance becomes possible. It can be a simple matter of contributing to a conversation or avoiding a question that you don't want to answer, as in the case of JFK's press conference ploy. Or it can be more complex, like detecting a possible lie. The principle is the same. You have to understand what's being said.

3. Recognizing inconsistencies between words and signals is a function of Spare Thinking Time—a

vital function, because inconsistencies provide the first disclosure that something is amiss.

Remember how important that first telltale smile was when I asked Archibald Harrison III about the $350,000 ripoff? Obviously his disclaimer of any knowledge of the theft was nothing to smile about, but its significance had to be recognized. Would you have spotted it?

All right, maybe you will never be confronted by a high-stakes crook like Archie. But you wouldn't want to forget Poker Player Number Five, who stroked his money when he liked his cards, never when they were bad. If you recognized that inconspicuous little trait, he couldn't bluff you. A valuable edge? Yes . . . and not only in poker.

4. Calculating your response in advance makes all the difference when you're at a disadvantage, as when asking your boss for a raise. Approaching any situation hat in hand can be damaging if you're unwilling to take the initiative.

While making your pitch to someone who has the upper hand, watch for the nonverbal response to what you're saying. If it's either positive or ambivalent, you know you have the option to forge ahead. If it's negative, you can change your direction or even your goal. What's important is awareness and control—especially when the issue is as sensitive as the amount of your salary.

Think about what you want to say, anticipate the boss's response before it is made, be prepared to react to it—control is pivotal even if the boss's first response is negative. Your calm and collected re-action could change the man's mind.

5. Sending signals of approval or disapproval will make your point more effectively than words, just as a picture is said to be worth a thousand words.

   At the used-car lot, my method of countering the salesman's aggressiveness was with Silent Signals: a shrug, a skeptical look, an accusatory question. Small things, but he gradually got the message that I wouldn't pay his first asking price, or his second. Only when he finally talked turkey did I give him a smile, a nod—and a sale. It's a reliable strategy.

6. Being tactful is thought of as a social grace, but mastery of tact is more sweeping. It doesn't nec-essarily involve diplomacy or even politeness. Again, it's mostly a matter of control.

   We've all said something that we wish we hadn't said, or have begun a sentence and instantly re-gretted it. That's what happened to Archibald Har-rison III when he barely managed to bite off an incriminating sentence in the middle.

   Archibald was so confident and surefooted that he stopped using his Spare Thinking Time. And there's the most important lesson of all.

   No matter how smart you are, if you want to match wits successfully, you can't waste any of your Spare Thinking Time. You'll never know when it will save you from making a mistake, but you can be sure of this much:

   Sooner or later, it will.

* * *

Here are a couple of simple exercises that you can work out on your own. They involve common situations that confront us all.

Just apply the six methods as numbered in each case.

EXAMPLE: A secretary tells you: "Mr. Smith is in a meeting right now. He should be out soon."

1. Was she smiling or prune-faced? Did she convey apology with a palms-up gesture? Or convey dismissal with a wave of the hand?

2. What did it mean that she said *should* instead of *will*—and did she stress the word *soon* or swallow it?

3. Was she looking directly at you as she spoke or fiddling with papers, denying your presence despite her disarming words?

4. Consider your options. Do you challenge her— declare that you have an appointment now? Or do you play it patiently? For how long?

5. Your response must be either prepackaged or contrived on the spot. In this case a smile plus a thank-you means you accept your fate; a frown plus a comment means you accept nothing. A mix (smiling snide remark or frowning thank-you) means "Okay, I know you're toying with me, but I'll wait."

6. Keep your poise. Obviously, that's much easier to do if you have thought it all out in advance.

EXAMPLE: A face-to-face confrontation erupts . . . in a traffic situation, at a ball game or a cocktail party, in a dispute over a neighbor's dog, even in a family quarrel.

1. Study your antagonist. Is he truly combat ready? Does he look aggressive or passive? Is he jockeying for position or standing still? Is he shaking his fist, or are his hands in his pocket? Is his face contorted or calm?

2. Is he making any sense, or is he just ranting? Are his words directed at you, or might he be angry over something separate from you—in effect, lying to himself? And how about you: is your own position justifiable?

3. Are his actions and his words consistent? If he is standing still, with a calm face, but ranting loudly, he's probably just letting off steam. If he's talking softly but in a combative stance and looking angry, be careful. He could be on the verge of physical assault—depending on your next word or move.

4. Calculate what you want to do before you do it. If you are not in physical jeopardy, you can pursue the argument. If the risk is too high, be prepared to withdraw.

5. Accompany your planned course of action with clear signals of what you intend to do—to avert any misunderstanding. In simplest terms, a nod announces that you are in some degree yielding. A shake of the head says the opposite. The goal is clarity.

6. Temper, temper. Lose it and you will lose. Control it and you win—assuming that the confrontation remains verbal. If there's physical combat, of course, both sides could become losers.

* * *

Finally, a word about the doubts you may have. I won't pretend it's easy to become skillful at using Spare Thinking Time. It takes determination and some confidence to master this strategy.

How can you be positive if you're negative? How can you have confidence if you lack it?

Essentially it's an exercise in talking yourself into something. It helps to do anything if you've done it before, but many things in your life are occurring for the first time.

In practicing strategies, create a hypothesis as to what could happen—and how you would respond to it if it did happen.

You still might not anticipate accurately, but even when you fail, you are highly likely to learn something useful.

Just don't give up. A loss is not always final.

You play the game until it's over.

CHAPTER

CLUE #5— SEARCHING QUESTIONS

SHE HAS BEEN OPEN AND RESPONSIVE FROM THE BE-
ginning, the kind of wife or lover you always wanted.
For a year you have been together, with never a discordant note.

But now, in the past ten days or so, she has become
more and more distant.

You want to find out what's wrong. The best way is
by talking.

"What's wrong?" you ask her as casually as possible.

"Nothing," she says tonelessly.

You talk about inconsequential things for a minute
or two—waiting to see if she lightens up. But she has
a hard time smiling.

"What is it?" you ask. She gives you a blank look.

"You seem distant. You're not yourself these days."

Is she straying? That's the question in your mind,
and the word *distant* suggests some sort of sexual rift.

But there's no point in accusing her, even if you're irritated. You want to keep the dialogue open, to remain calm enough to learn what's going on. Whatever the immediate problem, chances are it didn't cause the rift. People usually fool around because there's already a void.

If she's unhappy or angry—on the other side of a wall—the more you talk the more chance you have to knock down the wall.

She shrugs. "I'm okay," she says. "What do you want for dinner?" You spend a minute or two on that subject. You suggest her favorite chicken recipe and watch to see if that pleases her.

"All right," she says dully.

"I don't know what to suggest to you these days," you say. "I feel I'm losing touch with you, and I don't want that."

She closes her eyes.

"Please don't lock me out. I want to help."

She opens her eyes. They seem a little damp.

"We can work this out," you assure her. "Together."

And that's just what you intend to do. You're mentally prepared to look at the problem objectively—or even entirely from her point of view. That's what people find hardest to do.

Although you certainly wanted to know if she was straying, that thought was not put into words. None of the things you said were accusatory. None were hostile attacks that would deepen the conflict. Your approach was calculated to keep open a line of communication.

Most people do not approach this dilemma this way. But it is a formula that usually works.

Here are the ingredients, all part of the above scenario:

1. By design, as the first phase of the formula, your first questions used the neutral word *what*, signifying that something external was to blame, not she. Your purpose was to open up the subject calmly and offer her an opportunity to respond calmly.

2. In phase two of the formula, the thrust is on the word *you*—switching out of the neutral zone. While still not accusatory, it legitimately focuses on her as the center of the situation. Your purpose is to uncork her—to help her say whatever she has to say—so the problem can be solved.

3. The third phase introduces the word *I* for the first time, a reminder of the other participant in this situation. You're not saying: "Look what you're doing to me!" But if she's not going to talk about the problem from her own perspective, maybe she'll want to help you. Your goal is to open up a dialogue. You try every key.

4. *We* is the fourth phase, the perception that you and she can solve this problem together. The problem is a shared one—and the togetherness option is still alive.

It doesn't always open up the avenue to peace. There is no sure formula that always works. But the percentages are that this approach might work, whereas an angry confrontation has no chance.

There is always room to compromise. The bottom

line is: *maybe vs. never*. You can profit by it—in addition to extending your life expectancy.

I have been digging for the truth for most of my adult life, with and without a badge. But believe me, it doesn't have to mean giving someone the third degree. All it means is asking a series of questions. Anyone can do that.

For a detective grilling a theft suspect, the questions can be spoken quietly and calmly. But they will always follow a formula: direct, aggressive, zeroed in on the truth.

The sequence might go like this:

1. Do you know where the safe is?
2. Who else has access to it?
3. Have you ever opened the safe?
4. What reason do you have to open it?
5. Did you know money was in the safe?
6. Shouldn't you have known?
7. Were you anywhere near the safe that day?
8. Did anyone see you near it?

A personnel director interviewing a job applicant is less aggressive than a cop—and maybe less direct—but still searching for answers. He might ask:

1. Why did you leave your last job?
2. Did you like your boss?
3. Do you still have friends there?
4. Do you drink? Smoke? Do drugs?

You can see the formula—a series of questions designed to evaluate stability, personality, compatibility, or potential character flaws. The interrogation-interview may not produce a definitive portrait of the job applicant, but it's a start.

A series of questions will work the same way at a party or in any social situation when you get a reply ranging from ambiguous to unresponsive. But social niceties require you to go slow in a conversational interrogation. You have to be more courteous than the cop, more patient than the personnel director.

What's needed is a formula for digging gently. Not just serial questions but what I call *Searching Questions* . . . a subtle form of interrogation.

This is Clue #5 to catching a liar. The formula is a series of questions *to be asked in a logical progression* during a conversation.

Even if the first question or set of questions is inconclusive, the groundwork has been laid for a second set of follow-up questions to evaluate the first set of answers.

If necessary, third and fourth sets of follow-up questions can be asked with the same goal in mind.

Success usually doesn't take too much effort. The extent of your interrogation depends on your subject's patience, of course, but even more on your skill and energy.

The key to excavating the truth through Searching Questions is knowing what to watch for, knowing what to listen for—and, once again, identifying inconsistencies in the person's responses.

You explore the inconsistencies by returning—in due course—to the question that produced the inconsistencies. Again, go slow. It's wise to drop the subject of your question entirely for a while—perhaps more than once—because pressing a question can trigger resistance. Inconsistency is in itself a form of resistance, so tread lightly when you do return to your quest for the truth. Don't counterpunch on an aggressive basis; don't make it obvious. Just introduce new sets of Searching Questions as the conversation progresses.

Keep asking yourself:

1. Do the responses match?
2. Are the pieces consistent? If not, another set of questions is in order.

Let's see how Searching Questions work in an elementary type of social situation: trying to find out how old somebody is. It's a question that often brings an evasive answer, for either serious or frivolous reasons.

If you suspect a lie, here is an example of what course to follow.

First, drop the subject.

Then, listen for any conventional topic of conversation to arise—sex, politics, religion, money, education. Now begin to establish a time frame with Clue #5. It may only take one question to get your answer. It may ultimately take dozens of questions. What's important is the concept of a series of questions.

TOPIC: Sex.

First set of Searching Questions: "How old were you when you had your first date?" If the answer is fourteen, nothing in particular is revealed. But if you then ask what happened on that first date, and it turns out to have been a movie date, you can see the possibilities. ''What movie did you see?'' (That could be the last question of the first set.) If the answer is, say, *The Deer Hunter*, you have your first reference point. ''That must have been 1977, wasn't it?'' . . .

If your suspicions persist, or deepen due to any inconsistency in the response, just halt your search again and await a new opening.

TOPIC: Politics.

Second set of questions: How old were you when you first voted? For whom? Gerald Ford? Ah, he just missed by a few votes, didn't he? I remember that Carter election—what was it, 1976?

TOPIC: Money.

Third set of questions: How old were you when you got your first job? Doing what? Where? Did you stay long? Only until you started college? When was that?

Still suspicious? Drop the subject again, and wait.

TOPIC: Religion.

Fourth set of questions: Do you still go to church? When did you stop? At eighteen? Why? Because you got drafted—I see. Was that during the Vietnam war? But you must have missed the worst of the war, didn't you? Oh, 1970.

By now you not only have several markers on the trail you've blazed—you probably have a ballpark answer to your question. If your man was eighteen in 1970, he was born in about 1952.

That's an example of how it works in a simple scenario.

Now let us turn our attention to a much more complex situation.

No issue of our time has raised more questions than the spreading plague of AIDS—and no answers have been more elusive. But beyond the scientific and moral debates, one question is uppermost for ordinary people all over the world:

How do you find out if someone has been exposed to the AIDS virus?

The question is rarely asked directly because a *no* answer could be a lie, and that risk can't be accepted. So we dance around it.

We research the person's recent past with questions to determine the degree of monogamy . . . and that of his or her recent partners . . . and all of their sexual preferences . . . and their IV-drug histories . . . and their incidences of blood transfusions.

We listen hard to the responses, and watch for non-verbal signals—and inconsistencies. None of us who ask these questions about AIDS is oblivious of the lessons of this book. Our concentration is total.

The answers may not be definitive. Only laboratory testing can provide facts about the AIDS epidemic. But the answers to our Searching Questions can give us potentially vital clues.

Heavy sexual activity with a variety of partners would increase the chances that he or she had contact with someone with AIDS, no matter if the contact was infected sexually, by IV-drug use, or by any form of blood transmission.

So social conversations tend to run like this:

TOPIC: Sex.

First set of Searching Questions: Are you dating anyone special? When was the last time you got involved? What happened to that relationship? Was she the faithful type or promiscuous? Did she use drugs? What kind? Did you ever see her with a needle—or any of her friends? Was there anyone before her? How long ago? What about her?

Let's assume the man being interrogated sounds clean. The subject of his history is played out, at least temporarily. But the issue is far from dead.

TOPIC: Politics.

Second set of questions: What do you think of testing for AIDS? If they made testing mandatory, would you resist it? What should be done about people diagnosed as having AIDS? Should they be isolated? Your purpose here is to determine how seriously he regards AIDS. Let's assume he perceives the threat clearly. He still isn't above suspicion. When it comes to AIDS, everyone is a stranger.

TOPIC: Religion.

Third set of questions: How do you feel about using condoms? Have you ever used them? Do you have religious scruples? What's your opinion of the church controversy over condoms? Don't you believe birth control and protection against AIDS are separate issues? Do you think your objection to condoms might ever change?

By now—no matter how your Searching Questions were answered—you have a reasonably clear picture of what kind of person you're dealing with in terms of AIDS.

It's a narrow focus, and there may be many other variables, but at least you have enough information to play the percentages. You can estimate what the chances are that this person has been exposed to AIDS.

Be thankful that most social questions are less threatening.

Social situations can vary depending on who's involved—family, friends, strangers, foes. Individuals, even some that you know well, like spouses and siblings, can change, depending on the situation. But keep two principles in mind:

1. Identify your goal—the true answer to a specific question.
2. Have a plan for reaching that goal.

It doesn't have to be a complex plan. The simplest way to get a straight answer is to phrase a question so that it requires more than a yes or no reply. That gives you a chance to evaluate more than just one word. You can watch and listen to the total response—not only several words but also nonverbal signals.

Here are some examples of questions that can be

answered with a yes or no—and the same question designed to elicit fuller information.

DON'T ASK:	ASK:
All set for the meeting?	What did you prepare for the meeting?
Will you be here soon?	Where are you?
Is my car ready?	When will my car be ready?
Are you into cocaine?	How do you feel about using cocaine?
Did you finish your homework?	What's your homework assignment?
Are you lonely?	Why in the world are you sitting here alone?
Is that your bottom line?	What is your bottom line?

You get the point. Phrase questions to avoid yes-no answers.

As I have said, interrogation is my business. Searching Questions are a vital part of it.

One of the most memorable chapters in my career occurred when a tourist came to New York from Canada for a weekend of combined work and pleasure. It was a long weekend.

He was a thirty-three-year-old Quebec businessman named Pierre, a husky man, about six foot two and two hundred pounds, and very thirsty. Pierre and a group of friends got together in a bar and grew convivial. Later, back on the sidewalk, their good cheer erupted noisily. A policeman appeared. He singled out Pierre as the most unruly member of the group. An argument ensued, then a shoving match. Punches were thrown, and Pierre decked the cop. The friends vanished. Pierre was locked up.

He contended that the cop had started it, making fun of his French accent, calling him names, insulting him, and then shoving him.

The key question was who had thrown the first punch. I knew I would have to use Clue #5 to search for the answer.

Pierre was a little vague on that specific subject. He seemed either unwilling or unable to distinguish between a shove and a punch.

What made it unusual was that Pierre was no common street brawler. He was an influential executive—vice president of a Montreal firm—so the case was adjourned briefly, and he was released on his own recognizance to return home. While there, he consented in a long-distance phone call to return for a polygraph test—to help resolve the issue of who started the fight.

If he passed the polygraph test, the assault charge against him would be dropped. But that turned out to be a big if.

When Pierre returned, I noticed that he seemed anxious about the possibility that his boss might find out about his arrest. I made a mental note of that. It could come in handy.

Fear is a psychological weakness that regularly turns up in lie detection. People fear their parents, their spouses, or God. Or losing their job or social status. You try to isolate every subject's fear. It's his Achilles' heel.

Before his polygraph test, Pierre repeated his original version of events.

His whole story flowed out: the cop had called him names and ridiculed him . . . and insulted him . . .

and shoved him. Pierre spoke fluent English. He was very emphatic.

But when I came back to the specifics of who threw the first punch, there was a lot of hesitation and stammering—as if Pierre needed more time to think about his answer.

He talked with his hands a lot, waving them in the air. But each time I asked him about the first punch, his hands dropped.

His mouth movements varied, too. On most questions his upper lip pressed downward lightly on his lower lip. On punch questions, it was the reverse: the lower lip half covered the upper lip.

Could that be a sign of deception?

I hooked up Pierre to the polygraph. He took the test. He failed it.

In post-test interrogation, I told him he was a liar. But I acknowledged having some doubt about what really occurred.

"The truth might lie somewhere in between," I said. My purpose was to give Pierre some latitude, not box him into a corner.

Now I idly asked if his boss knew about the polygraph test. He shook his head glumly. "Well," I said—implying that I would keep it a secret—"if anyone is in a position to help you, I am. So let me help you. Let's talk."

As I continued my Searching Questions about the cop, about who had done what—about which of them had made the first physical contact, the first shove, the first punch—Pierre leaned toward me a little, nodding his head slightly. He was beginning to cave in.

Finally, he just stood silently. And I stood silently. Pierre waited. So did I. Almost always, in that situation, whoever speaks first loses.

"You're right," said Pierre.

"I know I'm right."

"What do you want me to say?"

"Just tell the truth."

He told it.

He had been drinking and had gotten boisterous, and the cop had tried to calm him down.

But the cop had been too polite. And Pierre, who was bigger than the cop, took the politeness as a sign of weakness. So he elbowed the cop away.

That's how it began. With an elbow.

"I never would have done it if I was sober," Pierre said.

The judge accepted that. The charge against Pierre was reduced to attempted assault. The six-month sentence was suspended. A fine was paid.

Case closed.

CHAPTER

■■■ 9 ■■■

THE DOUBLE CHECK

WHILE YOU HAVE LEARNED THE BASIC TECHNIQUES OF lie detection, there is also something of an art to it. And as with any art, it can't become simple until you know exactly what you are doing.

That requires thinking. It requires a reasonably open mind—free of illusion, preconception, and bias. It requires psychic energy.

Be exacting on yourself when it comes to interpreting words and Silent Signals. Don't take a little bit of knowledge and apply it carelessly. Use *all* you know.

Develop your own principles and methods of detection. Question assumptions, yours as well as others. The more deeply rooted the belief, the more carefully it should be examined. Check all the evidence.

And then double-check it.

When words and signals conflict, for example, the percentages are high that you need to ask some pointed questions. Don't jump to conclusions. Someone can say *yes* with a negative shake of the head, after all, and sincerely mean *yes*. People do get confused. Find out what the head shake means.

Until the answer is in and you are certain it's accurate, it is wiser and safer to keep an open mind.

Most schools don't teach you how to keep your mind open—to ask more questions until you have the correct answer. An occasional teacher makes the attempt, and it is often remembered with gratitude by a limited number of appreciative students. But schools in general attempt to dictate a wide range of beliefs.

Too often we don't bother to question them. And we don't shrug off this negative influence after graduation. We develop the habit of not asking questions. As a consequence we miss things that turn out to be important.

I remember one case vividly, no doubt because I am reminded of it by similar cases more and more often. It involved what had become a controversial issue after just one generation of the sexual revolution. The issue is forced sex in a social situation. It is commonly known as date rape.

It was a police case in New York, initiated by a young woman who charged that she had been raped on a first date. The man did not dispute most of the facts. He did challenge her interpretation.

Melvin was a businessman in his late thirties, recently separated from his wife and their two children. His social haunts were upscale, and he qualified as a respectable citizen. But perhaps most important, he thought of himself as a nice guy. Certainly not a rapist.

One night in a midtown Manhattan bar he picked up a twenty-four-year-old showgirl named Susan. They liked each other. And after hitting a few more bars, Susan took Melvin home to her Brooklyn apartment at 5:00 A.M.

Even in the Big Apple, that might still raise eyebrows. But Susan later said she didn't consider it a sexual invitation, because there hadn't been any of that kind of urgency with Melvin. They were just having a lot of laughs and good talk.

Originally from the Cincinnati area, Susan had worked as a belly dancer and was accustomed to the late-night club scene, so she had some experience at sizing up men. Melvin seemed like a decent guy. He hadn't made a pass at her in the bars.

But once inside her apartment, she said, he wasted no time.

Here is Susan's version of events:

As soon as she took off her coat, Melvin embraced her. She fended him off, explaining that her teenage niece from Ohio was asleep in the bedroom. "Oh, I'll fuck her, too," Melvin said.

His threat was not made in a menacing tone—"It was more passionate," Susan said. But for the first time, she was frightened.

Melvin apparently didn't notice her fear. He grabbed her by the hand, and Susan found herself being pulled down onto a couch, where he began nibbling at her neck. She made a mild attempt at resistance, which Melvin overcame by rolling on top of her. He pinned her arms and tried to unbutton her slacks. It was happening very quickly.

"No, stop, I don't want to do that," Susan said. "Leave me alone. You'd better leave!"

But instead of leaving, he put his hands around her throat and asked, "How would you like me to choke you?" By now, Susan was terrified. She went limp, and stayed that way, while Melvin proceeded to rape her.

There were no more laughs, no more talk. He just buckled his belt, straightened his tie, and left the apartment. It was daylight—the end of a shocking nightmare for Susan.

She thought about it for a half hour, wondering how she could have misjudged a man so badly, before deciding to go to the police. That in itself was a rarity, since most rape victims do not call the cops.

Susan knew Melvin's last name and the name of his company, so there was no delay in locating him. He was brought in for questioning on suspicion of rape.

His first comment to me was: "Are you kidding? Hey, she brought me home to her place at five in the morning!"

It is common enough in rape cases for the woman's behavior to be challenged—often by the public, by other women as well as men. But whether or not it had been wise for Susan to welcome a man into her home at any hour was not, of course, the issue.

The question was whether he had threatened Susan and forced himself upon her.

While Melvin denied it vehemently, he also wanted to avoid having the case put before a grand jury, with its potential for publicity. So he consented to a polygraph test, a chance to prove his claim of innocence.

In his pretest interview, Melvin's version of events was straightforward—until he got to questions about the niece.

Q. Who else was in the apartment besides you and Susan?

A. There were only . . . I don't . . . there were just the two of us. I didn't see anybody else there.

Melvin was sitting down during the interview, seemingly at ease. But during that start-and-stop response his hand went to his collar and unbuttoned it, and loosened his tie. He was visibly choking on his own words.

Q. Didn't Susan tell you someone was in the apartment?

A. Well, I didn't see anyone. . . . She may have. . . . Yeah, she did say somebody was there . . . her sister or someone.

Melvin shifted slightly in his chair.

Q. Let's put that aside. What happened at that point?

A. Her tongue kept protruding from her mouth. You know what that means, don't you? You've been around. I just took her hand and led her to the couch.

Q. Did she resist?

A. Well, you know how some women play hard to get. Hey, she didn't scream or anything. She didn't try to hit me or anything.

Q. Did you threaten to kill her?
A. Absolutely not.

Melvin was very relaxed again when he denied the threat. In his mind, he really hadn't threatened her.

Q. Did you put your hands around her neck and threaten to choke her?
A. I was making love to her. My hands were all over her body.

Melvin's hands started to move in the air, tracing the memory of Susan's body. But then his face turned away, a seemingly innocent gesture—except that his whole head turned completely away from me while he spoke. I thought that was significant—probably central, since he avoided any mention of Susan's neck. If he were telling the whole truth about where his hands had been, he would have acted more macho, proudly watching my face for some reaction. I decided to press the point.

Q. You don't understand the question. Did you put your hands around her neck and threaten to choke her?
A. No, I wouldn't do something like that.

I immediately administered the polygraph test. Melvin flunked it so badly that his veracity was destroyed. He knew it, too—maybe for the first time consciously.

In his post-test interview, responding to the same line of questioning, Melvin admitted that he had threatened to choke Susan. It didn't take long for him to confess that her accusation was true.

He was a father with a young daughter and a son. I think he wanted to believe that he had done nothing wrong, although deep down he knew better.

A classic case of date rape. It happens more often than most men—or women—are willing to admit.

I know some of you will still ask: Why *did* Susan bring a stranger into her home at 5:00 A.M.? It's a fair question. And I think the answer is fair, too.

There are a lot of different kinds of personalities in the world. I've known women, and men, too, who need companionship. They know it's not going to be a lasting relationship, but as long as it lasts, they want to savor it. And Melvin was a seemingly decent, mild-mannered guy. Susan could have expected him to take no for an answer.

What was his fate in court? Did he serve time? Well, rest assured that rape is a felony offense.

There are other men like Melvin out there. Let them think it over.

The truth goes undetected when no one is watching or listening, or asking questions. No matter what the evidence appears to show, double-check it. You can be wrong. Society can be wrong. The polygraph has demonstrated the innocence of many people regarded as guilty.

Obviously, polygraph tests are most often used to help establish guilt. But I unmask most liars simply by questioning them, since the polygraph has some practical limits. A test cannot be administered effectively without the subject's consent, and anyone can refuse to take it.

Even someone who feels compelled to take a polygraph—under pressure from the police, say, or from an employer—can deliberately distort the test and thus invalidate it. Anyone might thwart a test by holding his breath, for example, or constantly twisting and turning, or tightening the sphincter muscles.

But while it seems ironic, most people under suspicion will welcome the opportunity to have their honesty measured by electric impulses.

The guilty tend to assume that if they refuse a lie test, their guilt will become obvious—and a surprising number of guilty people believe they can beat a polygraph test.

For the innocent there may be the fear of the unknown—what the polygraph might reveal about their private lives or possibly a criminal past. But once it has been clarified for them that the test has a limited scope, applying only to the matter at hand, the innocent tend to consent willingly.

I will be brief as to the technicalities of how the polygraph works.

The basic instrument (there are several generations of models) is a metal box containing three to six instrument panels, each with a pen attached. The most widely used models have four pens.

Each pen, electrically linked to a separate measuring component, records a pattern of psycho-physiological activity on a moving chart.

Two pens record breathing patterns. They are linked to pneumonic tubes fastened around the subject's abdomen and chest cavity.

One pen is linked to electrodes attached to two fingers of one hand (usually the index and ring fingers). It measures varying levels of perspiration.

The fourth pen is electrically linked to a cuff—the type that doctors use—to monitor changes in blood pressure and pulse rate.

As you've seen in the movies, the patterns on the chart show rather vividly how a person responds to crucial questions.

But Hollywood, as it does in all aspects of real life, sensationalizes the lie test beyond recognition.

One reality is that there are no long-winded explanations during an actual instrument test. Questions are answered yes or no.

Until 1955 there probably weren't a hundred people in the United States who knew how to administer polygraph tests. But by the mid-sixties, private industry had begun to take a strong interest in polygraphy. It was triggered by a spectcular increase in retail and wholesale thievery.

Most such crimes are inside jobs, and despite mounting safeguards in a growing urban population, the theft rate has not abated. Nor has industry's alarm over its losses. In some states you can't get a job without a pre-employment polygraph test.

What is the success rate of the polygraph? That depends on who is measuring the rate—proponents or opponents of the instrument.

Perhaps 5 percent of all polygraph tests are inconclusive due to conflicting physiological responses or some form of distortion, whether technical or intentional.

Of the remaining tests, I estimate the accuracy rate at about 87 percent. It may range higher or lower, depending on the skill of the examiner—admittedly an important variable.

But remember, lying is proven (in this context) *before* or *after* a polygraph test . . . in the pretest or post-test interview phases, as I have illustrated in several vignettes.

You don't always get a confession, not even from someone who fails a polygraph test. But a confession is the goal, since polygraph results are open to challenge everywhere.

And in my opinion—with rare exceptions—a voluntary confession is the truth.

The key to lie detection is not inside the metal box. It is one-on-one observation and questioning that elicits either an admission or fresh information.

I once had a theft suspect named Alfred who didn't react physiologically to a polygraph test—a rare *nonreactor*. He had no pulse jump, no respiratory change, no sweat. His test was one of the five percenters—inconclusive.

But Alfred did react physically, with more than his share of nonverbal signals.

I first noticed something in his pretest interview. Alfred's most telling facial expression was what I call looking-up-to-the-heavens—as if to say "Help!"

He did it after denying that he had stolen more than $10,000 in cash and merchandise from the clothing store where he was an assistant manager. And I remember that beseeching look when his polygraph test produced nothing.

"Alfred," I said, "I'm going to tell you something that will make you very happy. Your polygraph test was inconclusive. But the bad news is that I've made my own subjective evaluation."

He tensed up.

I told him I didn't believe his story. There had just been too much physical activity—although I didn't tell him that.

He made no protest. Nothing. At first he just looked at me, like a basset hound. Then he asked: "What do you mean?"

"I mean I don't believe you."

"What do you think I had to do with it?" Alfred pleaded. He was cowering. He wouldn't challenge me, even though he had beaten the polygraph.

"I'm here to find the truth," I said calmly. "The truth is that you're involved in that missing money." I pointed an accusatory finger at him.

"I-I-I don't know what you're talking about," Alfred whispered.

Because he was panicky enough to stutter, I decided to back away from the stolen money. After all, I assured him, even if there were a lot of thefts, they were usually small amounts.

Alfred's body relaxed a little.

"Let's talk about merchandise," I said. "How many times have you walked out of the store with merchandise?"

Silence.

"Just tell me how many times—Ten? . . . Twenty? . . . Thirty?"

"Not that many," Alfred said. Then he gulped.

I backed off again—into the let-me-help-you routine. Then I reversed the numbers, minimizing everything.

"All right, it wasn't thirty. Was it twenty? . . . Fifteen?"

He shook his head slowly.

"Around ten times, right?"

"Well, yeah."

In the end he returned $3,600 in cash and more than $4,600 in merchandise. He had gotten the stuff out of the store in his attaché case. Most such retail theft doesn't turn up until an audit, and then it can be explained away as shoplifting. But Alfred had gone much too far—in more ways than one.

Why did he sit still for all my questions? I wasn't wearing my badge, and the polygraph test hadn't exposed Alfred. Why didn't he just get up and leave?

Because people who want to confess don't want to leave. I have escorted people out of my office, practically pushed them out the door, and they have walked back in to confess.

People who do something right have a deep need to talk about it.

And so do people who do something wrong.

KNOWLEDGE AND ETHICS

NOW IT IS QUESTION TIME. THERE ARE SOME VALID issues in the study of lie detection. Here are my responses:

Is there any intrinsic value in having such knowledge and applying it?

Yes. There's tremendous potential profit in knowing what you're doing.

In the lie-test field, that potential is rising. While polygraphy has enjoyed a decade of relative prosperity, the pendulum is now swinging against it. Critics who view it as an intrusion on individual liberty are moving to banish pre-employment polygraph testing from the workplace. Law enforcement testing will remain intact as well as specific tests in the commercial sector. Federal legislation is now in place supporting this position.

As opposition to the polygraph grows, skill at conducting one-on-one observation and analysis will take on a new dimension in the private sector. But regardless of its role in the business world, I believe the polygraph can be no more than a complement to the personal observation of Silent Signals.

For the individual, watching and listening with increased comprehension simply brings you closer to the truth. You make fewer mistakes in judging people and situations. You become wary of illusion created for effect—usually based on power, money, social status, education, or age. You never evaluate anyone purely on the basis of his position in the world. You no longer accept first impressions and make them final. You have more evidence now.

Knowing that the spoken word is merely the bare bones of the message—that the real meaning is more often in the delivery—turns up evidence not only when you suspect a lie, but when you are unsure. And my contention is that you can't afford to guess whether or not someone is lying.

Even when you're certain you've heard a lie, it doesn't pay to brand anyone a liar without examining all the evidence. First impressions are strong, and usually lasting, but you can contain the damage of a wrong first impression. Keep watching and listening. Give anyone—and give yourself—another chance. Maybe you heard wrong the first time. Maybe you misinterpreted a word or signal. Jumping to conclusions can be hazardous.

Words are tricky, you know. Someone will utter a Helium Word that stimulates a new line of thought, and then say something unplanned. A specific word can also befuddle. Say you are telling someone about a perceived injustice. He murmurs yes, and you stop. Did he mean yes, that's unjust, or yes, what happened was understandable? The word reflected his thinking, but it wasn't clear.

"What do you mean, yes?" you ask, searching for clarity.

In much the same way, maybe someone you deem a liar is not a liar but merely confused.

People do lie with regularity, but in this context it is not always a simple case of lying. People may delude themselves, or may have some other difficulty stating the facts, even when the facts are obvious or well known. And the delusion might be just temporary. How often have you heard someone say with a shrug: "I may have said that, but that's not what I meant."

Is that a lie? You need more evidence. He might be a person who had said something abusive and was now thinking better of it. Or maybe his mind was just wandering. You find a way to measure his sincerity.

How can you know the difference between genuine and false sincerity?

Most people who try to fake sincerity can't do it. As the number-one quality of successful politicians, it is evidently a rare commodity. There have been superstar pols, of course. But think of how few.

You might assume that any trained actor can fake things—even something as basic as sincerity. But consider the tiny percentage of actors able to find work. It's not just the breaks; you need believability. If role-playing or sincerity is fraudulent, the audience reaction is usually negative. Not always, but it adheres to percentages. Sincerity is not often read wrongly.

It becomes easier to read, of course, when you are familiar with a person. With someone new, an unknown quantity, explicit signals can be totally absent. You have to be especially alert for Silent Signals from relative strangers. Think of what you see and hear as feedback.

As a corollary, how many times have you waited in vain for feedback—someone to tell you that what you're doing is correct and that you should continue in that course of action? How often has someone known you were headed wrong—and didn't tell you?

If you are not in a position to ask direct questions for any reason, at least you now have the ability to observe. Watching and listening for nonverbal communication results in receiving messages consciously—eventually making nearly every message conscious.

It's like learning how to watch a baseball game at the age of six. You raise your consciousness notch by notch.

Does skill in lie detection become a burden?
No, you can shut it off, then draw on it at will.

It's a bank. You have many deposits of know-how in your brain that remain dormant until needed. Identify and utilize the skills that work for you. Many people need to be taught that they have strengths lying dormant. Locked into mundane work, you can lose sight of the fact that you have inborn skills. If you recognize your strengths, it can change your life.

What are the ethics of lie detection? (Is it fair to tell a lie in order to expose a lie, as you did with Archibald Hamilton III?)

In polygraph examinations of criminal suspects it's allowable because you have an overriding objective: to identify the guilty person. That's my opinion. I don't say all lies are unjustified.

Is a lawyer morally justified in tricking a jury? In European courtrooms it is done without an outright lie, merely with a gesture. Few American law schools offer courses in body language, so deceit is more flagrant. In either setting, however, my answer is both yes and no.

Whom is the lawyer defending? What if it's a major narcotics smuggler? A known rapist? What if the client is truly innocent but jeopardized by a hostile court? While I know this is tantamount to asking whose ox is being gored, I shrink from hard-and-fast rules. An alternative to weighing the ethics issue here would be to draw a distinction between using power for good or evil.

The issue of intent applies to much of what you have learned here. A lot of lie detection techniques put you in an advantageous position. It might be deemed fraudulent to control situations, for example, by deliberately sending certain signals. But intent would be a decisive element. I see nothing fraudulent if conscious signals are sent for ethical reasons.

You have considerably more knowledge now, however, about one important aspect of human behavior. And to the degree that knowledge is power, it can indeed corrupt even in small ways. It matters how you choose to use any advantage that you now have.

The moral obligation lies with you.

ABOUT THE AUTHORS

Former detective WILLIAM J. MAJESKI is a twenty-one year veteran of the New York City Police Department. Concurrently, for fifteen years he has been a polygraph examiner for both law enforcement groups and private industry. Over the years he has conducted thousands of interviews, interrogations, and polygraph tests. He has used his expertise in numerous investigations—the most notable one concluding in the capture of Jack Henry Abbott. Mr. Majeski holds a Bachelor of Science degree from John Jay College of Criminal Justice and is a graduate of the F.B.I. National Academy. He is a teacher of polygraph science and has been an adjunct professor at Long Island University. The owner and operator of a security company in New York, he also lectures and conducts seminars.

RALPH BUTLER was a news and sports writer and editor at the *New York Post* for thirty-one years.